T0302937

Michael McIntosh

MORE

SHOTGUNS

AND

SHOOTING

Michael McIntosh

M O R E

SHOTGUNS

AND

SHOOTING

Illustrations by Bruce Langton

THE DERRYDALE PRESS
Lanham • Boulder • New York • London

THE DERRYDALE PRESS

Published by The Derrydale Press
An imprint of The Rowman & Littlefield Publishing Group, Inc.
4501 Forbes Boulevard, Suite 200, Lanham, Maryland 20706
www.rowman.com

16 Carlisle Street, London W1D 3BT, United Kingdom

Distributed by NATIONAL BOOK NETWORK

Copyright © 1998 by Michael McIntosh
Illustrations © 1998 by Bruce Langton
First Derrydale Printing 2014
This Derrydale Press edition of *More Shotguns and Shooting* is an unabridged republication
of the edition first published in Selma, Alabama, in 1998 by Countrysport Press.

Most of the chapters in this book first appeared, in somewhat different form,
in the following magazines: *Shooting Sportsman, Sporting Classics, Gun Dog,
The Double Gun Journal,* and *Field & Stream.*

The book was designed by Saxon Design, Traverse City, Michigan. It is set in Bembo,
which is modeled on typefaces cut by Francesco Griffo in 1495. It is considered one of the
first of the oldstyle typefaces that were used as staple text types in Europe for 200 years.

British Library Cataloguing in Publication Information Available

Library of Congress Cataloging-in-Publication Data

The Countrysport Press edition of this book was previously catalogued
by the Library of Congress as follows:

McIntosh, Michael.
More shotguns and shooting / Michael McIntosh ; illustrations by Bruce Langton.
p. cm.
Includes index.
1. Shotguns. 2. Fowling. I. Title.
SK274.5 .M388 1998
799.2/028/34   98043589

ISBN 978-1-58667-147-1 (cloth)—ISBN 978-1-58667-150-1 (electronic)

To October First
June 21, 1983–September 8, 1998
to whom guns meant adventures
and shooting meant birds to retrieve, now and then
and to Vicky
for being my anchor.

Contents

PART II: SHOOTING—MORE CRAFT, CARTRIDGES, AND CONTROVERSIES

CRAFT

CARTRIDGES

CONTROVERSIES

PART III: ODDS & ENDS

Preface

I've always had rather mixed feelings about sequels. It's natural to want more of something good, but sequels often end up being diluted versions of the original. Much as I enjoyed *Rocky*, I'd be more than a little skeptical about *Rocky XXVII*. On the other hand, I reach for *Gough Thomas's Second Gun Book* as often as I do the first, and if he'd chosen to call the next one *Gough Thomas's Third Gun Book* instead of *Shotguns & Cartridges*, I'd like it just as much. I wish the dear old soul had lived long enough to write a fourth and a fifth, just as I wish Gene Hill was still with us to write a sequel to *Shotgunner's Notebook*. Some subjects are so rich and varied that the vein never seems to peter out.

I had no notion of a sequel to *Shotguns and Shooting* when it was published in 1995. Yet here it is—for the same reason Gough Thomas cited in his preface to the *Second Gun Book*: "My justification for compiling it must rest on the generous reception of the previous volume by critics and readers."

For my part, I must reverse the order. The critics certainly have been kind to *Shotguns and Shooting*; I'm grateful for that, but it's the readers who've made the real difference. Literally dozens have told me they found *Shotguns and Shooting* both enjoyable and useful, and that reaches to the heart of why I continue to eke out a living in the word trade.

The chapters of *Shotguns and Shooting* were written over a period of about ten years. The ones presented here cover about a four-year span and represent my continued delving into both the technical and practical aspects of the gun. Though most of the subjects are completely different from those in the previous volume, a few either expand upon old topics or approach them from another angle. Shotguns are an enormously complex subject, but yet so thoroughly integrated that virtually every aspect somehow touches every other. This in itself is part of the fascination.

The most obvious similarities between these two books are in the section on shooting, although I've expanded the scope and the details of the shooting method I teach far beyond where the earlier volume leaves off. You'll notice, as I did when I actually put these pieces together, that I keep coming back to a few basic principles—point the gun, extend your leading hand, move that hand first, keep your head dead-still. I'm sorry if it sounds repetitious, but those are the key concepts, and I know from a lot of teaching experience that anyone who wants to be a better shot can't hear them too often.

In all, this is yet another celebration of the gun, and if, as Gough Thomas did, I have deliberately sought out some of the "less well-trodden paths of shotgun lore," it's because they lead ultimately back to the familiar places we love the best.

Sanctuary Ridge
Custer, South Dakota
October 1998

Acknowledgments

As with the previous volume, these chapters first appeared in magazines, and as always, I'm grateful to the editors whose skill, taste, and friendship mean so much to me:

Silvio Calabi, Ralph Stuart, and Vic Venters of *Shooting Sportsman*; Chuck Wechsler of *Sporting Classics*; Bob Wilbanks and Rick Van Etten of *Gun Dog*; Daniel Coté of *The Double Gun Journal*; and David Petzal of *Field & Stream*.

Bob and Susan Hunter of Countrysport Press deserve many thanks, not only for their friendship and continued support but also for their tireless efforts on behalf of keeping a once-sinking ship afloat.

If you find this a handsome volume, it's because Angela Saxon, who has designed so many of my books, is a wizard at making such things look their best and because Bruce Langton is as good a sporting artist as you'll ever find.

Once again, I wish I could name everyone who has taught me something about guns and shooting; it was an impossibly long list before, and now it's longer still. But I owe special thanks to my friends and colleagues Jack Mitchell, Bryan Bilinski, and David Trevallion. Without them, I could still be a writer, but I wouldn't have nearly as much to say.

To Tober, for fifteen years of devotion. Rest easy, old girl; if there are no birds to bump in Heaven, then there is no Heaven.

And to Vicky, just for being.

Part I

SHOTGUNS

MORE LOVE, LORE,

AND LEGEND

LOVE

1

THINKING OF WHERE WE'VE BEEN

I have no idea where the notion came from, nor why it struck me then and there, but it stayed on my mind for a long time after.

I took my favorite gun out of the case, hooked the barrels to the frame, and snapped the fore-end into place—something I've done so many times that I can do it in my sleep. The active part of my mind, or what's left of it, was occupied with the flock of birds waiting in a willow brake a few dozen yards away. Nothing odd about that, either.

But then I looked at this gun in my hands, and for one instant everything else fled away. For that moment there were no birds, no companions, no weather or light, only a single certainty all intact and shining, clear as a neon sign on a darkened wall: If the people who made this gun knew where it was and what I'd been doing with it, they'd be spinning in their graves.

The thought blinked out after a few seconds, and we went on about our birdy business, but the feeling stayed with me, like the afterimage of a flashing light. The more I turned it over, the more bizarre the situation seemed.

There I was on a gravel bar along the Copper River in Alaska, as wild as any piece of country I've ever seen, surrounded by bear tracks and about to shoot spruce grouse with a shotgun built in the capital city of the British Empire more than a generation before I was born.

We who love them are fond of wondering what they'd say if these old guns could talk, enough so that the expression itself has almost become a cliché, one of those trite little phrases despised by every Freshman English teacher who ever lived. Which is okay for them, but there's something to consider: Clichés become clichés because they're true, because they express some significant perception in a way that no other words can capture quite so clearly.

So do I wish my guns could talk? Damn right; especially this one.

Every gun that's not spanking-new has a story. Some of them probably are boring as haircuts:

Well, I've been in this closet for about thirty-five years, gathering dust and the smell of mothballs...and before that I belonged to a guy who went pheasant hunting once every season, on opening day....

Others must crackle with adventure and great tales of long ago:

He was the best shot in the county, loved to hunt...did some market gunning every fall, after the crops were in. There were ducks and shorebirds and prairie chickens back then, and passenger pigeons, you just couldn't count 'em...

Between, like the filling in a homemade pie, lie the stories we all know something about, of love for wild things and places passed down from one generation to the next, of guns that became symbols of responsibility, badges of emerging adulthood, talismanic emblems to the rites of passage.

The fact is, we and our guns help define one another. Without us to give them purpose and use, they are merely objects, just as a wedding ring without a hand is nothing more than a metal hoop, devoid of meaning. Without our guns, we cannot be hunters, cannot truly participate in the vast natural cycle that operates in the continuous tension of life and death.

As human lives sometimes take odd and unexpected turns, so, too, do the stories of the guns that go with us. And that's what struck me so strongly there on the Copper, realizing for the first time what profound contrasts exist between the world where my old gun was made and the one it lives in now, between the shooting it was made for and the shooting it's done since. It is by no means unique in all of that, hundreds of other guns have been more places and shot more birds than mine and in fact, I know only a fraction of this gun's history, only the few years we've been together.

Even so, we've had some times.

This old gun came into being twenty-nine years before I did, in 1916, precisely at the mid-point of the terrible war that changed the world forever. It was built in a workshop at 1 Rose and Crown Yard, London, at the lower end of St. James's Street just off Pall Mall, by men who belonged among the finest gunmaking craftsmen the world has ever seen. Barrelmaker, actioner, ejector man, stockmaker, polisher, finisher, and others, they're all gone now, all but lost in the forgetful fogs of history. Perhaps someday, when I'm in London with time on my hands, I'll be able to turn up a few of their names; until then I will know them only through the gun they left behind.

Whoever they were, they worked that summer almost within sound of the cannons battering Europe, building my gun and another just like it while their sons and brothers and friends died in muddy trenches. The record shows that the guns were made for Mr. J. Ross Saunders Price. Whether he was the actual customer or an agent, I don't know, but whoever ended up with them was a man of sufficient means to pay the then-princely sum of £100 for a pair of best London guns.

"Best" applied to the materials as well as the quality of work. The locks came from Joseph Brazier of Wolverhampton; at the time, best Brazier locks were among the finest in England. Sir Joseph Whitworth's firm made the barrel forgings. Whitworth steel tubes were the barrels of choice among the top British makers; Purdey's, for example, used them exclusively from the early 1880s until Whitworth's went out of business, well into this century.

Despite the craftsmanship and the pedigree conferred by the component parts, these guns were completely unremarkable in the context of their time. Nowadays, in the gun rack at a shoot almost anywhere in the world, they'd likely catch your eye; in England during the 1910s and 1920s, they wouldn't have earned a second glance among the Purdeys and Hollands and Bosses and others. There and then, best London guns were the norm, not the exception.

Those were to be the last, fading days of a once-vast empire. Following a terrible toll of lives lost between 1914 and 1918, economic hardships plagued England in the early 1920s. Still, though reduced in scope and lacking the luster of earlier times, the sporting traditions continued, and there's not a doubt in my mind that my old gun took part.

Virtually any game guns built as a pair were meant specifically for driven shooting—pheasant, partridge, and in the north, red grouse—a formal, elegant and thoroughly wonderful form of sport that reached full flower around the turn of the century. Influenced by the tastes of Albert Edward, Prince of Wales and later King Edward VII, driven shooting was the milieu of the wealthy class, performed on vast estates in an environment of formal dining and costume balls, supported by small armies of loaders, gamekeepers, beaters, stops, pickers-up, and others. It was a stage upon which brilliant shots performed—Lord Ripon and Lord Walsingham and the Indian Black Prince, Duleep Singh, while others, all in exquisitely tailored tweeds, did their best to shoot competently and with impeccable manners. What times those must have been.

Though the elaborate shooting parties were almost gone by the 1920s, most of the great estates were still intact, and I have to wonder which among them my gun and its companion may have visited—Elveden, Holkham, Blenheim, Studley Royal, perhaps even the Royal Family's own estate at Sandringham? Maybe some, maybe none. I'll never know.

Nor will I know when the two guns parted company, only that they did possibly during the 1930s, when England suffered almost as much as we did from the effects of the Great Depression. At any rate, by the early 1950s my gun, one of the pair, belonged to a gentleman named B. McMahon. I can only guess what the "B" stood for, but I'm sure he pronounced his surname in the Irish fashion, *MAC-ma-hone*. His initials were on the stock oval and the lid of the oak-and-leather case when I got them.

Similarly, I have no way of knowing how or when the gun made its way to this country, but somehow it ended up with a dealer in Tennessee and from thence to me.

The opportunity to own and shoot a best-quality London gun represented the fulfillment of a long-cherished dream. Beyond that I had no particular intentions apart from making it truly my own, by which I mean having the stock dimensions and handling dynamics tailored to fit.

A gun can become an intensely personal item. Shared experience is part of it, and so is a custom fit, but there's another dimension as well, which comes from having it worked on by people who are both master craftsmen and good friends. The feeling is hard to explain, but maybe it doesn't need explanation. Maybe it's enough to say that during a one-week period in the summer of 1991, I watched my dear friend David Trevallion turn a French walnut blank into a new stock for my gun, refining the fit down to a gnat's whisker and applying all the craftsmanship he's learned over more than forty years in the trade, first at Purdey's and since as an independent stockmaker. To me, the result is more than just a best-quality stock.

Another good friend took a hand in it as well. A few months later, Marcus Hunt engraved my initials and a dog-tooth border on the stock oval. Both Marcus and his sister Alison learned the craft from their father, and you can see from their work that Ken Hunt is not only the finest engraver in England but no slouch as a teacher, either.

While I'm sure the men who built it would fully approve of what's been done to it since, I have a notion they'd be at least bemused, if not bewildered, by some of the places I've taken it and some of the birds it's shot. Pheasants they would certainly be comfortable with, and woodcock, possibly even ruffed grouse, although they might raise an eyebrow at some of the alder swamps and popple hells in Ontario and Michigan and Wisconsin and Minnesota where we've gone to find them.

Some of those men might have known about Southern American quail hunting. If so, I suspect they'd recognize something in the traditions of mule-drawn wagons and stylish dogs as similar in spirit to their own shooting traditions. Blue quail in the black brush of south Texas, however, would probably seem to them as alien as the far side of the moon, and yet their gun has been there.

It also has been to the plains of Montana, the hills of Colorado, and the prairies of South Dakota, and has killed sage grouse and sharptails, gray partridge and blue grouse, mourning doves, chukars, prairie chickens, even snipe. It's been from sea-level to the mountains, from the desert to the tundra.

Their gun has ridden in airplanes large and small, in jeeps, pickup trucks, Range Rovers, democrat wagons, boats, all manner of automobiles, and even in a couple of saddle scabbards. It's been with me while I was dressed in breeks and a necktie, and at other times in old canvas shirts softened by a zillion wash days, and brush pants so frayed and patched that you couldn't pay the Salvation Army to accept them. It's been in my hands when I've shot as well as I can shoot and so poorly that I couldn't hit a two-hole outhouse if I was locked inside.

I wish I could sit down with those long-ago men and tell them how I feel about the gun they built, how much it means to me, what pleasure it's given, how grateful I am to have it. I'd like to describe to them all the lovely places it's been and the beautiful birds it's put into my hands. I like to think they'd accept most of it with good grace, but Alaska, I don't know. They might consider that the last straw and get exasperated with me:

"Now see here, old man; that's going a bit far, don't you think?"

Matter of fact, I do. It's far in time and space, but no farther than a lot of other places I never thought I'd get to be.

And, I would have to tell them, if the red gods are willing, it's not over yet.

2

IN PRAISE
OF DINOSAURS

Among the dozens of photos, mementos, and assorted bric-a-brac hanging on my gun-room walls is a photograph of Gene Hill shooting doves in Mexico with a hammer gun. If memory serves, it's a 28-bore built around the end of the last century by John Blanch & Sons of Gracechurch Street, London. It's also a gun for which I harbor a case of covetousness that would make Midas blush. Gene loved it right up to and beyond the point when some scuzzbag stole it from him. Gene was as loony about hammer guns as I am.

This is for the most part a harmless, if slightly eccentric passion. In the face of current technology, a hammer gun may seem as old-fashioned as high-button shoes or a manual typewriter, but to my eye there's no more elegant firearm than some sleek old beauty tricked out with a set of swan-necked hammers. It doesn't much matter to me whether she's wearing back-action locks that taper gracefully down the hand of the stock or the more modern-looking barlocks; if she's a hammer gun built to high standards of the craft, she'll have my complete and immediate attention.

The English hammer gun, or one made elsewhere after the English pattern, arguably represents the ultimate perfection of the breechloader. It can have every feature of a hammerless gun including ejectors and a single trigger, although relatively few were built with either one, and it offers some things that hammerless guns generally don't.

Because they don't have to accommodate large internal tumblers, a hammer gun's frame and lockplates can be smaller, which serves both to reduce weight and to create a slimmer profile. Moreover, the hammers themselves and the area of the fences where the strikers protrude allow lockmakers and actioners vast opportunity to show just how artistic they can be with chisels and files. Study a top-quality piece and you'll find it sculpted in an astonishingly complex symphony of curves and planes.

The most common indictments leveled against hammer guns are that they're slow, clumsy, and essentially unsafe. Granted, the hammers take some getting used to, but with a little practice you can easily develop the knack of cocking both at once with your trigger-hand thumb; it takes a bit more time than simply flicking a safety button, but once you get the hang of it, the difference is scarcely more than a few milliseconds. And if you're shooting doves or ducks or birds over pointing dogs you'll usually have plenty of time anyway.

As to ease of handling, I can thumb back a pair of hammers just about as smoothly as I can press the cross-bolt safety on a pump or autoloader and with a lot less fumbling than I can work that godawful left-side mounted safety that W.W. Greener and a whole bunch of German and Austrian makers apparently thought was the niftiest thing since canned beer. And if I can get accustomed to hammers, anybody can.

I don't see anything inherently unsafe about a hammer gun, either. In fact, I'd argue that in the hands of a shooter who has his wits about him a hammer gun is actually safer than any other. A hammerless gun is always cocked, and its safety system is no less liable to failure than any mechanical device. Drop the gun or otherwise subject it to a sharp blow and it's apt to go off despite the safety. Most best-quality sidelocks have interceptors that prevent accidental discharge, but those can break, too.

There are two completely safe ways of carrying a hammer gun. One is to leave the hammers down until you're ready to shoot. If it has rebounding locks that are in sound condition, it'll take a very hard blow to break the safety notch on the tumbler and drive the hammer against the striker, a harder blow, I suspect, than would jar off a hammerless lock.

Another way is to carry it with hammers cocked and leave the action open until you intend to fire. When it's open, the strikers can't reach the primers, no matter what. The only trick is to be damn sure the muzzles are pointed safely as you close it and not slam it shut as if you were breeching a cannon. Handle it, in other words, just as you'd handle any gun.

Considering the mechanisms involved, it seems to me that a good craftsman shouldn't have any great difficulty making and installing a typical trigger-block safety on just about any hammer gun. It would require welding an extension to the top strap and some skillful fitting and inletting besides making the parts to begin with, but it certainly could be done. I intend to have a gun so converted sometime, just for the hell of it.

Action-open is also the way to uncock the locks, holding each hammer in turn with your thumb and easing it down. The mainsprings are strong, and a hammer-spur can slip off your thumb, but there's no possible danger so long as the gun's open.

One of the best of all things about hammer guns is that they can be had for relatively little money, typically less than half the price of a comparable hammerless gun by the same maker. Finding good ones can take some doing, but they're out there. This is especially true of English guns, somewhat less so of

European pieces, and much less so of those made in the United States. The American trade built very few hammer guns after the turn of the century, and not many have survived in shootable condition. Importers such as H & D Folsom Arms brought in thousands of cheap hammer guns between about 1880 and the first World War, and these were marketed under dozens of different trade names. Most were built in Belgium, most have long since fallen apart, and virtually none of the survivors are safe to shoot nowadays. If you run across a piece that bears a name you never heard of, is stamped with Belgian proof marks, and looks cheaply made, it's a wall-hanger, not a shooter.

The same, unfortunately, is generally true of really good-quality guns bearing such venerable names as Parker and Lefever and others. The problem lies mostly in the barrels. The hammer gun's heyday was also the heyday of twist barrels, which were meant for black-powder cartridges. The Damascus barrels on American guns which most makers purchased from Belgium and England may or may not be safe with nitro powders, but as the United States has neither a national proof house nor any uniform standards of proof, the only wise thing to do is assume they're not and never fire any modern cartridge in a twist-barreled American gun. Or send it to England and have it nitro-proofed.

The majority of English and European hammer guns also have Damascus barrels, but a substantial number of these were proofed with nitro powder. On English guns, look for stamps showing the letters NP or BNP under either an arm and sword or a crown, and usually the words NITRO PROOF as well. You want to see these regardless of whether the barrels are twist or solid steel.

It's also comforting to see a reproof stamp—the letter R under a crown—which means the gun has gone through one of the English proof houses a second time since it was new. And even if it has, you'll want to have the barrels examined and measured by a professional who knows English guns before you plunk down good money and cork off the first shot.

If all this is too difficult to accomplish and you still want a hammer gun to shoot, you can get one brand-new from Italy. Bertuzzi builds lovely hammer guns, both self- and manual-cocking and fitted with tang safeties. They're expensive, as much as $10,000 or more, but they're exquisitely made. On a more economical scale, Bernardelli makes hammer guns in a couple of different models from about $2,500 up.

You should expect to pay at least twice that for a hammer gun by Purdey, Boss, or Holland & Holland, maybe three or four times more, if it's an especially nice piece. On the other hand, you can find some splendid guns by lesser-known makers at splendidly lesser prices. I recently came across a 12-bore by William Richards of Liverpool that was a steal at just over $3,000 and I'll long rue the fact that my disposable income wasn't up to the strain just then.

Besides the aesthetics, there's a historical element as well, something wonderfully Victorian about a fine old hammer gun. I can hold one and imagine I've gone back a hundred years in time, perhaps to shoot on one of the great country estates in the company of Lord Ripon, who was the finest game shot in England. It's said that Ripon could time and again have six pheasants dead in the air at once using his set of three Purdey hammer guns and two loaders, guns he continued to use long after everyone else had gone hammerless. He was shooting them, in fact, on the day he died, in 1923.

Having shot a few birds with hammer guns myself, I think I know how the old boy felt about them. They may be dinosaurs in this age of computer-driven automobiles and cellular phones, but put a good one in my hands and you'll never see anyone happier to kiss a lizard.

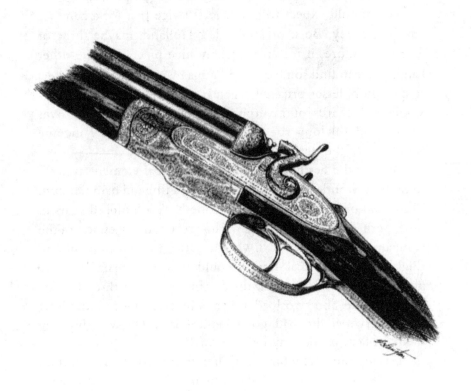

3

BACK TO
THE FUTURE

A gun has no voice with which to sing its own song, no words to tell its own story. A pity, that, because there are stories beyond counting locked mutely behind those insensible barriers of wood and steel. Epic tales, odd happenings, romantic yarns, spellbinding or mundane, no matter; every gun could tell us something, give us some window or mirror to history.

Which is not to say that such stories are beyond all grasp, only that it's our job to tell them. Sometimes the facts are easy to uncover, sometimes all but impossible. Sometimes the rewards are greater than others. Once in a while what emerges is astonishing, both in its symmetry and in the chimes of history that start to ring. Thus it is with a certain Purdey.

In this story, the middle is as good a place as any to start. That's where I came in and where it began to unfold, forward and backward all at once.

In June 1991 a friend called from Colorado, a gun dealer who had word that a small collection was going up for sale—two dozen pieces from the estate of a man recently deceased, offered on bids by his widow. As they were located not far from where I lived, he asked if I'd hire on as his agent for a day, go look them over and report back on their nature and condition.

There were some interesting items in the bunch: a Westley Richards Ovundo droplock, a hammerless Woodward with a snap-action under-lever, a couple of W & C Scotts, a nice boxlock ejector gun by K.D. Radcliffe of Colchester, a 20-bore hammer gun by William Ford, a bar-in-wood Army & Navy hammer gun, a Clabrough 8-bore hammer gun, a Tolley 8-bore rifle, a German double rifle rebarreled by Westley Richards in, of all things, .32-40, and so on.

But the one that captured my heart—and made me a bit sad as well—was a Purdey hammer gun. As I described it in the notes I typed up the following day:

"Purdey No. 10615, c.1879; 12-gauge hammer gun, top-lever, bar-action locks; non-ejector; No. 2 of a pair; 30-inch Whitworth barrels; London reproof at .740"; 2½" chambers, 3-ton proof; rib address 314½ Oxford Street.

"Miller single trigger, sequence left-right; restocked in very bland walnut, quality of work excellent but doesn't look like a Purdey should, much too thick and chunky; fore-end original, quite worn, steel diamond insert replaced with brass; metal of frame and locks in good condition; engraving Kell-style small scroll, condition very good; screws slightly burred; barrels reblacked, rib engraving faint, ring well."

I sent the notes off to Colorado and put the whole thing out of mind except to wonder at odd moments how that poor old Purdey, obviously once a magnificent example of Victorian gunmaking, ever came to such a sorry state, and to wish I could have seen it before it got buggered up. I've had similar thoughts about a lot of guns.

A few days later I took off for Maine to spend a week with my old friend David Trevallion and work a stockmaking story. One day in the shop, I mentioned the collection I'd seen and said, "There's a top-lever hammer Purdey in there that'd make you cry. Got a Miller trigger and the clunkiest damn stock you ever saw, just butt-ugly."

David looked up from his work, then at me. "Do you remember the number?"

"Yeah, ten-six-one-five. Somebody oughtta be shot for what he did to that gun."

David put down his chisel, went into his office and hauled open a file drawer. A minute later he came back and handed me a sheet of thick paper with some black-and-white photos pasted to it and a series of notes written along one side. I'd seen such pages before; they're how he used to keep record of the guns he stocked.

And there was Purdey No. 10615, Miller trigger, ugly stock and all.

"You made that??" I was flabbergasted and half-embarrassed all at once—sort of like telling somebody about an especially ugly woman you've seen and finding out it's his wife. It came as no surprise that David had worked on the gun; as the only Purdey-apprenticed stockmaker in the United States, he's probably worked on most of the English guns in the country over the past thirty years. But for him to have made that stock fairly blew me down.

David grinned. "Yep, under protest, but I did it, just as the customer wanted. Read the notes."

Down near the bottom of the page he'd written: "Stocked with plain French wood to match Lingle's new Italian hammer gun. LOOKS BAD." That made me feel a little better.

"The original's over there," David said, pointing to a rank of old stocks hanging on the far wall. "It's the hollow one, the one you like."

Well, I'll be damned. To call it the one I like grossly understated the case. To me it is possibly the single most gorgeous piece of walnut ever put onto a gun, a visual feast of classic honey and smoke. It caught my eye the first time I set foot in David's shop and has done so every time since.

For the rest of the week I kept staring at it, trying to visualize how lovely that old gun must have looked. And to think it once had a mate, another gun just like it, with a stock sawn from the same plank... I finally decided that to dwell on such thoughts was courting madness and forced myself to stop.

I did okay for about a year and a half, until David said over the phone one day, "Oh, by the way, ten-six-one-five turned up at an auction a couple of weeks ago. Corry and I went together and bought it. It's here in the shop, and I'm thinking about putting her back the way she was."

That did it. I can get pretty sticky about hammer guns to begin with, but the notion of that one restored to original set my story-detector abuzz. And quite a story it turned out to be.

They were pigeon guns, Nos. 10614 and 10615, built on an order placed in 1878, and in several ways they represent the emergence of Purdey guns into the modern age.

For one thing, 1878 was the year Purdey's began exclusively making barrels of Sir Joseph Whitworth's then-new fluid steel, a tradition that continued virtually unbroken until well after World War II. (The sole hiatus came during the last five months of 1898, when British steelworkers went on strike and Purdey's barreled eighty-three guns with tubes obtained from Krupp.)

Chopper-lump barrels were not yet the London standard in 1878, and the barrels of Nos. 10614 and 10615 are made in the dovetail or dropper-lump style. The barrelmaker's name is one thing we still haven't turned up, but his initials were C.F.

The order originally called for narrow, tapered ribs, but this is crossed out and replaced with "new ⅜" + ¹⁄₁₆" wide Pigeon rib. Gold front bead."

They were among the first Purdeys built with solid-bar actions, as opposed to the earlier bar-in-wood style in which the stock extends under the action bar nearly to the knuckle. The frames are stamped "J&T.S"—which probably means they came from John and Thomas Sharp of Court 3 Whittall Street, Birmingham, who from 1877 to 1890 supplied fully or partially finished actions to the English trade.

The lockplates are stamped "IB," indicating that the locks were made by Joseph Brazier of Wolverhampton. For many years, well into the twentieth century, nearly all the best London makers used Brazier locks. These carry the additional stamp "Joint Patents, Stanton & Co. C31686*." The number probably was Brazier's in-house pattern or inventory designation, because the patent in question is No. 367 of 1867, issued to John Stanton, also of Wolverhampton and the father of the rebounding gunlock.

The stocks are specified at 14½ inches in length with 1⅜ inches bend at the face and 2⅛ inches at the bump. Give them about an inch more length and some cast, and they could have been made for me. The order called for steel heel and toe pieces, gold oval, and a gold diamond inletted to each fore-end meaning that what I first took to be a replacement piece was original after all.

When these guns were built, Purdey's factory was at 37 North Row, Avery Row, south of Oxford Street, just west of New Bond Street. Seventy-four workmen labored there under the direction of Mr. Wheatley, whose high-handed manner had earned him the nickname "Sheriff." Mr. Jones made those lovely stocks, and Mr. Apted finished both the metal and the wood.

The record says they were test-fired using cartridges loaded with three drams of black powder and 1¹/₁₆ ounces of shot. They weighed six pounds, eleven ounces each.

David sent a close-up photo to Ken Hunt, who confirmed that the engraving was done in the shop of Thomas Sanders and Henry John Kell, at 6 Greek Street, Soho. And the timing was one of those exquisite little junctions of history: Late 1879, when these guns were on Kell's bench, was when he and his wife conceived Henry Albert Kell, who would be born the following year, who would eventually become the preeminent English engraver of his time and who would train the current reigning master, Ken Hunt.

James Purdey the Younger, son of the founder, was head of Purdey's then, presiding over a front shop at the 314½ Oxford Street premises once occupied by his father's mentor, Joseph Manton. At the time, a best-quality Purdey gun cost ₤65 to ₤70, and delivery took about eighteen months.

In January 1880, Mr. Purdey handed his customer one of the loveliest pair of pigeon guns the firm ever built and received in payment the sum of ₤136.10s. Normally, best Purdeys would be housed in an oak-and-leather trunk; in this instance, the record mentions a Macintosh case.

On longstanding policy, Purdey's never reveals customers' names, but whoever the gentleman was, he was a picky sort. Two months later, in March 1880, he sent both guns back to have their stocks shortened by three-sixteenths inch, to "14¼" + ¹/₁₆"'' as the record book says. For this he paid one pound, sixteen shillings and sixpence.

The guns survived the next forty-six years without appearing in any record that has shown up so far. But in November 1926 Mr. C.F. Burrows brought No. 10615 back to Purdey's with its right barrel "injured 6 to 8 inches from the front." Whether Mr. Burrows owned the pair or whether they'd parted company by then is impossible to say, but No. 10615 was on its own thirty-three years after that, when W.J. Holliday, Sr., found it for sale at Westley Richards (Agency), 23 Conduit Street. Wherever it might have been during its seventy-nine years, it ended up just a few blocks from the North Row factory where it was built.

Holliday was chairman of W.J. Holliday & Company steel mills, a great pigeon and target shot, and founder of *Trap and Field* magazine—a wealthy man with a taste for fine guns. (He would later own the first Purdey that Ken Hunt ever engraved with game scenes.) On April 14, 1959, he paid ₤70 for Purdey No. 10615 and gave ₤4 more for "packing in a light wood box, postage and insurance" to have it shipped home to Indianapolis, Indiana, U.S.A.

Once there, he sent it to the Miller Single Trigger Manufacturing Company in Pennsylvania with orders to replace the original double triggers with a single, and specified that the non-selective mechanism be set to a left-right sequence, which he preferred for pigeon shooting.

Holliday kept the gun until 1968, then sold it to his friend and fellow pigeon shooter Fritz Gierhart. In 1970 Gierhart sold it to another pigeon man, Jim Nankevelle, bought it back the following year, then sold it to David Trevallion, who had a shop in Indianapolis in those days. In May 1971, Herter's Inc. CEO Bowman Lingle bought it with the provision that David would make a new stock in the image of an Italian hammer gun Lingle had recently acquired.

"He wanted the gun to be stock-heavy," David told me. "That's why the stock's so beefy. By itself, it weighed a pound and eleven ounces without a gold oval, and it made the gun stock-heavy by four ounces."

Lingle sold 10615 a year later to an Ohio dealer who sold it to a Chicago dealer who sold it to the man whose widow put it up for sale in 1991. Eighteen months after that, a Massachusetts dealer put it up at auction, and it went back to Trevallion's workshop.

And there it came full circle, back to where it started 115 years before.

First went the Miller trigger, replaced by new double triggers that David made on the pattern of the originals. The original stock, which at that point had been hanging in David's shop for twenty-two years, had been shortened again at some time; the heel and toe pieces were gone, though you could see the plugged holes for the screws that held them on, and the butt was simply finished off and checkered. And from the hand to the butt-plug it was completely hollow, the result of an experiment.

"Years ago, somebody wanted to know how much weight could be taken out of a stock," David says. "I was curious myself, so I grabbed an old stock and started boring it out. Just happened to be that one."

In the end, he'd taken out 7½ ounces, and the stock weighed only ten ounces, with its original gold oval still in place. He kept all the shavings, sealed in a plastic bag to show customers what was possible and also because Trevallion Gunstocks' Latin motto, if there was one, would translate as "Never Throw Anything Away." Which in this case proved a blessing, because now all those shavings are back inside the stock, mixed with Acra-Glas to form a solid mass once again.

Not surprisingly, the wood shrank a bit in all those years of just hanging around, so some of the inletting had to be deepened slightly to make everything fit the way it should. And considering that David inherited a fair number of tools passed down through generations of Purdey craftsmen, some of the chisels he used to do that might be the same ones Mr. Jones used in 1879. There's no way of knowing for sure, because chisels have no more voice than guns, but a few of David's are old enough that it's at least possible.

What's important is that 10615 now wears her old original stock once again, lengthened out with buffalo horn, which is how Purdey's would have done it a hundred years ago, and fitted with heel and toe pieces like she once had. Her locks have undergone some restorative surgery to repair the ravages of having been single-triggered, and her action joint is newly tightened. After a thorough cleaning, the engraving is almost as crisp as it was when Henry Kell cut it.

As another intertwining of history, David had Ken Hunt's son Marcus recut the original name and address on the top rib and cover the engraved "No. 2" (which some clod had obliterated with a center punch), with a small gold damascene, which means that No. 10615 got some re-engraving by the son of the man who learned the craft from the son of the man who did the original engraving. Not even a Russian novelist or a soap-opera scriptwriter could come up with interrelationships more complex than some that exist in the gun world.

The sister gun, No. 10614, is also in the United States, but as it was restocked with Monte Carlo and pistol-grip and single-triggered at Purdey's years ago, there's no chance it can ever be restored to as nearly original as No. 10615 now is.

But having one of the pair is enough, especially as it's back in shooting order as well. So far, David and I have put nearly a case of modern 2½-inch cartridges through the old girl. She shoots beautifully, and I'd give several important parts of my anatomy (important to me, anyway) if she were mine. She's altogether as sleek and graceful as the day Mr. Purdey handed her over. He was one of the last Purdeys who was a working gunmaker and no doubt felt a particular sense of pride in the guns he delivered that cold January day.

He deserved it. Hers is the kind of ageless beauty that defines our concept of quality at its best, and her odyssey proves that past and future can sometimes be all the same.

4

MORE, OR LESS, THAN MEETS THE EYE

If you know any practical gunmakers—members of the dirty-hands crowd who actually build the guns that are sold under the names of corporations or men who go to work in business suits—and want to provoke an instant rise, simply pick up any highly decorated gun, look it over, and say, "Now this is a fine gun. Just look at that engraving."

Depending upon the nationality of the man you're with, you might not understand the response, but it's guaranteed to translate as something like, "%@#$&&!! #$@&ing engravers don't make guns!! Gunmakers make guns!"

Which of course is absolutely true, but that doesn't stop us from appreciating engraving or from wanting our guns to have some, maybe even a lot. The fact is, man has felt a compulsion to decorate his weapons ever since the first Stone Age hunter painted colors and designs on the shaft of his spear. The

professional warrior of medieval times and before was an itin-
erant sort who took his pay straight to the nearest goldsmith
and had it inlaid or damascened on his armor and sword, thus
making his accumulated wealth both portable and attractive.

A further fact is that no other item of human manufacture
combines usefulness and artistry to the same extent as a beautifully made and decorated firearm. It'll defend your life and
fill your belly and delight your eyes all at once.

For several hundred years, from the beginning of firearms
till the flintlock era was nearing an end, decoration meant
carving and inlay on both wood and metal. Engraving, as such,
didn't become widely popular until the eighteenth century, and
for the next hundred years, the standard approach was what's
known as "open work," bold filigree that amounted to graceful
curlicues much like the adornments of old-style calligraphy.

Modern engraving first appeared in England in the 1860s
and '70s, a result of the Victorian penchant for elaborate decoration, and it derived directly from both architectural embel-
lishment and contemporary fashions of jewelry engraving. If
you want to see where traditional scroll engraving came from,
with its intricate, circular motifs, you have only to study
Victorian watch-backs, brooches, serving trays, and such.

Which is hardly surprising when you realize that until the
twentieth century there were no such creatures as full-time
gun engravers; there were jewelry engravers who also decorated guns and gun engravers who worked on jewelry during
the slack periods of the year.

Just as the guns created by the London trade during the
last half of the nineteenth century became the patterns and
standards by which guns everywhere have since been built
and judged, it's hardly surprising that their modes of decoration became world standards as well. Until the 1970s, "gun
engraving" meant "scrollwork," either small scroll with its minute
curls, or large scroll, also circular in shape but bolder in execu-
tion. Small scroll traditionally is combined with blossoms for
an overall pattern commonly described as "rose and scroll" or
"bouquet and scroll." Large scroll is typically augmented with

leafy designs—acanthus and grapevine and other such foliage. Each makes its own demands. Small scroll is more intricate, but large scroll takes longer to execute properly, because it has to be shaded to give it depth and dimension.

The first generation of English engravers to make names for themselves in the gun world began with Thomas Sanders, a jewelry engraver who set up in business on his own in 1862. Sanders trained Henry John Kell, who in turn trained his son Henry Albert Kell, now considered the master gun engraver of two generations past. Social trends that began in the 1870s created an enormous demand for fine guns, and the Kells found themselves in the right place at the right time.

John Sumner was a contemporary, and rival in the trade, of the younger Kell. After Henry Albert succeeded his father as owner of the business, his employees earned a measure of fame in their own right, among them, Bill Smith, Jim Jones, and Billy Ecford, who later became chief engraver at Holland & Holland.

Kell's apprentice Ken Hunt is the current reigning English master engraver. Others now in high demand include Ken's son Marcus and daughter Alison, Philip Coggan, Alan and Paul Brown, Ken Preater, Keith Thomas, and others.

Other gun trades had their own national styles of decoration and maintain them still. The heavy, Baroque-style carving from Germany and Austria is distinctive, as is the Belgian school, which evolved from Jean-Théodor de Bay in the sixteenth and seventeenth centuries to Felix Funken and Hyppolite and Lyson Corombelle in the early twentieth and Philipe Grifnee of current times.

Although the Italian school of engraving, centered in the gunmaking capital of Brescia, has been active for 400-odd years, only in the past twenty has it made a significant impact upon the gun world of western Europe and the United States. On the other hand, "significant impact" understates the fact by an order of magnitude, because the Italian artisans have in those two decades elevated gun engraving to a level undreamed-of a generation ago.

For English and German and Belgian engravers, art has traditionally lain solely in the abstract shapes of scroll. What figures, human or animal, appeared in their work were little more than caricatures, stick-figures, or rough shapes meant to suggest a game bird or a hunting dog. Have a look at the birds common to American double guns manufactured in the nineteenth and twentieth centuries, and you'll see what I mean. Most of the American engravers working in the trade till fairly recently were English- or European-trained, and while their scrollwork ranged from passable to excellent, their birds and dogs were invariably cartoon-simple.

The Italians changed all that and changed it for good. Through the work of Firmo Fracassi, Angelo Galeazzi, Gianfranco Pedersoli, Giancarlo Pedretti, Claudio Cremini, and a host of others, today's standards of gun engraving are to past levels what the special effects of *Jurassic Park* are to those of *King Kong*.

The Italian masters' scrollwork is flawless, though no better than the work you'll see from the Hunts or the Browns, Coggan or Winston Churchill or a score of others. Rendering figures is where they made their mark, with the engraving technique known as bulino.

It's so called from the *bulini*, the small, hand-held gravers used to perform the work, and it derives from the old craft of engraving stone tablets and metal plates used to print banknotes, stock certificates, and other highly ornate, highly detailed documents. Under the hands of a master, bulino is virtually photographic, so minutely detailed and lifelike that it's hard to believe the illusion is not reality.

But the reality is impressive enough, particularly when you know that bulino is neither etched nor transferred but rather cut, line by microscopic line, every cut raising a sliver of steel and combining in a series of halftones as subtle as the emulsion of a black-and-white photographic print. It is, in a word, incredible in its realism. It's what prompts surface-viewers to effuse at tedious length and declare any gun, whether jewel or gaspipe, a masterpiece of gunmaking based on decoration alone.

I certainly appreciate the skill that creates it, as I can appreciate any well-executed piece of graphic art, but as decoration for guns, bulino leaves me cold. It's not that I don't like images of birds and dogs and such; it's that I don't care to have them reproduced in every hair and feather, and especially don't care to see them on guns. I know what guns are for, and don't need pictures on them to remind me that dogs point and birds fly.

Non-sporting scenes that range from mythology to recent history and nude portraits leave me even colder, not of themselves, mind you, but as gun decoration. I haven't the slightest objection to seeing a grove-full of naiades capering in the altogether, but I'd far rather have them framed on my office wall than desporting themselves across the lockplates of a gun.

I'm a scroll guy, and whether it's small scroll or large makes little difference, so long as it's well executed. I know that no engraver ever made a gun go bang, filed an action, or fit a stock, and I have no illusions that a beautifully decorated gun is anything other than attractive junk unless real gunmakers built it. But I like engraving nonetheless.

As some writer observed years ago, it doesn't make a gun shoot any better, but it does give you something nice to look at when there's nothing to shoot.

LORE

5

Barrel Flip

I have an abiding fondness for shooting men and women who challenge conventional-wisdom shooters whose experience tells them that light loads are better for upland hunting than super-duper whomp-your-butt-in-the-dirt magnums; that guns with long barrels handle better than guns with short ones; that there is no universal prescription for "proper" balance; and so on.

One such shooter wrote to me some time ago, having read a piece I'd written on stock fit in which I mentioned that side-by-side guns generally need slightly higher stocks than over/unders because the muzzles of a side-by flip downward as the gun fires. "I've read similar statements before," he wrote. "Is this a proven fact or just another mythical hand-me-down?"

The letter I wrote in reply was, of necessity, the short answer; this is the long one.

Muzzle flip is a proven phenomenon. Rifle guys know it well, though they generally call it barrel flip, which actually is a more accurate description. As Major Sir Gerald Burrard puts it in *The Modern Shotgun*, "The flip of a barrel consists partly of a bending, just as a fishing-rod bends when an angler strikes, and partly of a vibration set up in the barrel...by the actual movement of the projectile down the bore."

The physical forces at work here combine Newton's law of equal and opposite reactions with the harmonic vibration created by driving a solid object down a long tube at high velocity. The same thing applies to guns as well as rifles. A barrel, even one firmly fixed to a solid receiver, flexes and hums when you fire something through it.

What Burrard never quite gets around to pointing out is that the mechanical nature of a break-open action adds an element of its own that accentuates the phenomenon.

Burning powder generates gas that exerts its force in all directions. Because a cartridge is enclosed in a thick-walled chamber that's sealed at the breech-end, the only available escape-route is down the barrel. That's how all firearms work.

But gas pressure still goes in all directions, and even though gun design thwarts the effort in every direction but one, the force naturally acts upon the gun itself. In a break-open gun, it literally urges the action to rotate on its hinge.

This pulls the barrel breeches slightly away from the action face, and that's one reason why guns eventually go off-face if you fire them enough. It's also why top fasteners on the order of Westley Richards, A.H. Fox, L.C. Smith, and others are so effective, and why the angle of the action, where the bar meets the standing breech, is a critical point. Take away the fasteners, and your side-by-side becomes a self-opener every shot; add the fasteners, and every cartridge you fire flexes the action bar a wee bit.

Have a close look at a few side-by-sides, regardless of who made them or when, and you'll notice that the junction of action bar and standing breech is always filed to a radius, never a square corner. It's done that way to lend strength at the frame's weakest point and it's why big side-by-side rifle frames often have bolsters at exactly the same place.

Combine this action-opening tendency with barrel flex and harmonic vibration, and you have a situation in which a gun muzzle dips significantly between the time you pull the trigger and the shot charge leaves the barrel. Both the physical reaction and the effect of recoil will make it rise afterward, but the important point is that barrel flip sends the center of the swarm angling low right from the start, and even though the deviation is minute at first, it increases geometrically with distance. At forty yards, it can amount to a foot or more.

If you want to see the whole thing in action, draw a one-inch dot on a patterning plate, back off forty yards or so, and carefully aim your side-by-side at the dot as if you were shooting a rifle. Try to get your line of sight as nearly parallel with the centerline of the bores as possible, scrunching your head down so you don't see any rib. You may not get it exactly right, because ribs aren't usually laid parallel to the bores, but you can get close. (You're also apt to get a rap on the cheekbone, doing this, so use the lightest load you can, and remember: It's all for science.) Shooting from a sandbag rest will accentuate the effect even more.

Then fire at the dot a second time, this time mounting the gun and cheeking it as you normally do, and you'll see a big difference in the two swarms' points of impact.

In the first instance, you're demonstrating what muzzle flip does to the shot charge and, in the second, how the height of the stock comb compensates for it.

Although muzzle flip affects all side-by-sides, the actual degree of it varies somewhat from gun to gun. Long barrels dip more than short ones, partly because shorter barrels are stiffer and partly because the muzzles of long barrels are farther from the chambers and therefore describe a greater degree of arc. Burrard makes the point, rightly, that if you rebarrel a 30-inch gun to 25 inches, it'll shoot higher than it used to.

Because over/under barrels are much more rigid vertically, they don't flex and they aren't as affected by harmonic vibration. Moreover, as the centerlines of the bores, especially the lower one, are much nearer the horizontal plane of the hinge than in a side-by-side, the rotational effect is considerably less.

But over/unders flip nevertheless—upward, so they tend to shoot high. In fact, if an over/under is decidedly butt-heavy and barrel-light, the whole gun wants to jump upward, which can leave your cheek feeling as though you've gone a couple of bad rounds against a middleweight with a snaky left hook.

This, incidentally, is not a problem that affects only short, lightweight guns. In the late 1960s I did my trapshooting with a 30-inch Winchester 101 that was a joy to shoot until I had it restocked with a much prettier, and much denser, piece of wood, at which time it became one of the most vicious cheekbone-pounders I ever shot. I finally figured out the problem and had the new stock bored out to put it back in balance, but not before I developed a flinch curable only by a solid month of not shooting.

Porting the barrels of an over/under reduces recoil-induced muzzle jump, but it doesn't entirely mitigate flip, simply because the barrels are already rising by the time the shot charge reaches the ports and some gas is able to escape.

The only effective way to compensate for flip, regardless of what type of gun you're dealing with, is by adjusting the stock. This is almost entirely a matter of bend, or drop, though cast is sometimes involved as well.

Bottom line is that flip happens, and because it happens in different ways from one sort of gun to another, applying the same stock dimensions to your side-by-sides and over/unders will likely have you flipping out, wondering why one or the other doesn't shoot where you look.

6

Recoil
& Kick

Firing a gun often makes me think of Isaac Newton. Having my mind on an Englishman who's been dead for 260-odd years instead of on whatever I'm trying to hit may explain why I shoot the way I sometimes do, but as alibis go, it's better than most.

Sir Isaac, you recall, was the one who first articulated the principle of physics that says every action prompts an equal and opposite reaction.

We rehearse the phenomenon, properly called Newton's Third Law of Motion, every time we pull a trigger. The force that drives the shot charge down the barrel also drives the gun in the opposite direction. Then the gun collides with some portion of our anatomy, principally the shoulder, and we absorb the impact. Two distinct cases of action and reaction.

The first instance, shot going one way and gun the other, is recoil, which is a simple physical response and precisely measurable.

Pure recoil is expressed in terms of velocity and energy, the same terms we use to describe the ballistics of shot and bullets, and they mean the same things in describing recoil. Velocity is how fast a gun moves in response to a fired cartridge; energy is how much force it subsequently transfers to whatever it hits.

Computing these values is relatively easy, thanks to formulae devised years ago by Julian Hatcher, of *Hatcher's Notebook* fame. If you find tinkering with math amusing, here's how to do it. You'll need an accurate pound scale to weigh your gun and a handloader's powder scale to weigh shot, powder, and wad. You'll also need to know the nominal muzzle velocity the cartridge delivers.

As a help, I've made up a couple of reference charts on page 53. One converts the standard shot charges from ounces to grains; the other lists nominal muzzle velocities for the standard factory loads most useful to an upland hunter. If you roll your own shells, you'll of course find powder-charge weights and muzzle velocities in your loading manual. If you're working with factory cartridges, you'll need to cut one open and weigh the powder and the wad.

Computing recoil velocity is the first step, and it's done by this formula:

$$\frac{(E+1.75P)Mv}{W}$$

$$7000$$

E is the total weight of the ejecta shot charge and wad in grains. P is the weight of the powder charge in grains. Mv is the muzzle velocity of the load. W is the weight of the gun in pounds.

As an example, let's assume we want to know how much recoil velocity a standard 3-dram, 1⅛-ounce 12-gauge load generates in a 7¼-pound gun. The shot charge weighs 492.1 grains and the wad 40.8 grains, so the value of E is 532.9. The powder charge weighs 20.5 grains; this we multiply by 1.75 to account for the fact that gases from the burning powder are moving faster than the shot when it leaves the muzzle. In this case, 1.75P amounts to 35.875.

Adding E and 1.75P gives us 568.775. Multiply that by the muzzle velocity, 1,200, and the result is 682,530. Dividing this by gun weight, 7.25, leaves 94,142.068. Finally, to reconcile the two units of weight we've used, divide by 7,000 (there are 7,000 grains to the pound) to find that this load sends this gun recoiling at the rate of 13.45 feet per second.

Once velocity is known, we can figure recoil energy with the formula $\frac{1}{2}MV^2$. In this, M represents the gun's mass: its weight in pounds divided by the acceleration of gravity, which is 32.2. V is recoil velocity multiplied by itself, in this case 13.45 x 13.45.

The mass of our 7.25-pound gun is .225. V^2 is 180.902. Multiply the one by the other to get 40.702, and divide in half to determine that this combination of load and gun generates 20.35 foot-pounds of recoil energy; enough energy, in other words, to lift a 20.35-pound object one foot against the pull of gravity. Or to put it another way, it's the force with which a one-pound object would strike if it was dropped from a height to 20.35 feet.

By comparison, an eight-pound rifle in .30-06 firing a 180-grain bullet at 2,700 feet per second generates recoil velocity of 12.73 feet per second and recoil energy of 20.13 foot-pounds. As the 3-dram, 1⅛-ounce round is the standard 12-bore target load, it's not hard to understand why a lot of old trap and skeet shooters flinch at the mere thought of pulling a trigger and tend to answer the phone when it isn't ringing.

Because recoil is a straightforward physical phenomenon, it responds to variation in logically predictable ways. Changing the value of any factor changes the end result. Fire identical loads in guns of different weight, and the heavier one will respond with less recoil velocity and energy, simply because it offers more resistance to the force driving it backward. And the differences are all proportional. Fire the same 12-gauge load we talked about earlier in an 8½-pound gun, which is 15 percent heavier than one that weighs 7¼ pounds, and both recoil factors are reduced by 15 percent. It works the other way, too; reduce the gun to six pounds (roughly 17 percent), and the recoil values of that load increase by the same proportion.

The same holds true of variations in powder charge, shot charge, and velocity. Increase or reduce any one of them, and the recoil values go up or down, accordingly.

Theoretically, if gun and cartridge case were the same weight as the shot charge and wad, it would recoil at the same speed as the shot's moving when it clears the muzzle. How's that for a shivery thought?

Fire a 3-dram, 1⅛-ounce load in an 8½-pound gun, and the recoil velocity and energy are less than in a 7½-pound gun, simply because the heavier gun offers more resistance. By the same token, though, a standard three-inch Magnum 20-gauge load—3-dram, 1¼-ounce—sends a six-pound gun recoiling at better than 17 feet per second with almost 29 foot-pounds of energy. That's almost exactly the same recoil you'd get from a .358 Winchester Magnum firing a 200-grain bullet from a rifle of the same weight.

Popular wisdom has it that small-bore guns recoil less than big ones, but as a general statement this is not necessarily true. Bore size alone means nothing compared to the weight of the gun and the load you fire in it. As W. W. Greener puts it in *The Gun*: "The gauge and length of the barrel will determine the weight of the weapon; if its weight is not proportionate to the load used, it will recoil unpleasantly. A safe rule is to have the gun 96 times heavier than the shot load. This means a 6-lb. gun for an ounce of shot; 6¾ lbs. for 1⅛ oz.; 7½ lbs. for 1¼ oz, and these may be shot with comfort irrespective of the gauge of the gun."

For the most part, Greener is right about this, but to my mind these are minimum weights, not necessarily the ideal for comfort. A few shots fired in a day's hunting is one thing, but shoot a couple of hundred 1⅛-ounce trap or skeet loads in one day with a 6¾-pound gun and you're likely to feel as if you've been stomped by a buffalo. On the same theme, the standard 3¼-dram, 1¼-ounce 12-gauge pigeon load doesn't recoil severely in a 7½-pound gun but if I'm going to fire fifty of them in the course of a twenty-five-bird race, it'll be in a gun of at least eight pounds.

On the other hand, if you can avoid the fallacy of thinking you need heavy loads for game birds or that flinging more pellets into the air will somehow make you a better shot, you can reap all the delights of a lightweight gun. My favorite 12-gauge game guns both weigh 6½ pounds. They're pleasant to carry and not uncomfortable to shoot with 1⅛-ounce loads at 1,200 feet per second, although the recoil is substantial—15 feet per second, with 22.5 foot-pounds of energy.

Except for pheasants under certain conditions, however, no upland hunter needs more than an ounce of shot, and my favorite one-ounce recipe turns out handloads that recoil at 13.39 feet per second with 17.93 foot-pounds. But for doves and grouse and woodcock and quail, ⅞-ounce of shot is plenty, and my pet recipes for those loads recoil my guns at 12.08 feet per second and give me only 14.6 foot-pounds of energy to deal with.

Use a gun that's lighter still and the load becomes even more critical in terms of recoil. We've already seen what a three-inch shell does to a six-pound 20-bore. With a standard target load of ¾-ounce of shot at 1,200 feet per second, the 28-gauge is a pussycat; recoil velocity in a 5½-pound gun is 11.82 feet per second, energy 11.88 foot-pounds. Even the so-called heavy field load—2¼-dram, ¾-ounce—isn't bad: 12.88 feet per second velocity, 14.10 foot-pounds energy.

But feed your wee 28 one of those godawful one-ounce Magnums and the pussycat comes back at 14.7 feet per second to wallop you with more than 18 foot-pounds of whack. That's almost 30 percent more than the recoil you'd get from the hottest .30-30 factory round you can buy if you fired it in a 5½-pound rifle. "Unpleasant" doesn't even begin to describe the experience of corking off two or three boxes of them in a light gun. Personally, I'd rather go fifteen with George Foreman.

This brings us to the point where pure recoil becomes an altogether different phenomenon. Put a shooter behind the gun, and recoil becomes kick. Some writers call it "felt recoil", which is perfectly accurate. I think of it as kick because that's just how it feels. By any name, though, it isn't nearly as simple or as easy to measure.

Recoil itself is solely a function of gun weight and load, but the way we perceive it is influenced by all sorts of factors: the mechanics of the gun, the inner contours of the barrel, the shape of the stock, the shape of the shooter, how well or poorly the gun fits him, how he holds it, how he reacts physically and psychologically, even the noise a gun makes.

It's the one thing every shooter has to deal with every time he fires a shot. No two shooters react in exactly the same way to kick in general, and we often react in different ways from one shot to the next.

Kick is partly in the gun, partly in the way we handle the gun, and partly in our heads. Kick is the price we pay for the pleasure of shooting. One axiom of economics has it that the price of anything shouldn't be greater than the return. In shooting, it goes a step further: the less we have to pay, the more pleasure we get.

The phrase "reduced recoil" gets tossed around the shooting world pretty freely. Sometimes it's meaningful, sometimes not. As we've seen, how much a gun recoils—that is, how much velocity and energy is involved—depends entirely upon the relationship between the weight of the gun and the load in the cartridge.

Nothing else affects actual recoil. Thoughtful handloaders are always on the lookout for recipes that produce relatively low chamber pressures. This is a kindness you can do for your gun, but don't get the notion that less pressure means less recoil. Hatcher's formulae prove that equal shot charges moving at equal velocities generate equal recoil. Fired in the same gun, an ounce of shot leaving the muzzle at 1,200 feet per second creates exactly the same recoil velocity and energy regardless of whether the chamber pressure is 10,000 units or 6,000. In fact, using a slower-burning powder to reduce pressure actually works up more pure recoil, because you have to use a heavier charge of it to get the same velocity. As the difference is very slight, you may not notice more kick, but you certainly aren't getting any less.

Much the same is true of long forcing cones, overbored barrels, and ported muzzles, all of which are fashionable at the moment, especially among sporting-clays shooters. Long, gradually tapered forcing cones and oversized bores do seem to produce more evenly distributed patterns, but they don't truly diminish recoil—unless, of course, a barrel is bored large enough that some gas is able to escape past the wad, which lowers the velocity of the shot charge, and also tends to wreck the pattern. Porting reduces muzzle jump, which may change the sensation of kick, but actual recoil remains the same.

Still, it's the sensation of kick we're concerned with, and while recoil reduction is one thing, recoil absorption is quite another. Anything that absorbs a significant amount of recoil energy before it's transferred from the gun to the shooter reduces the intensity of the kick. This might be as simple as a recoil pad or as complex as a mechanical system like the Hydrocoil, Counter Coil, Edwards Recoil Reducer, or some other.

It might even be part of the nature of a gun itself. Autoloaders kick less than guns with fixed breeches, because some recoil energy is used up in operating the action. Gas-operated autoloaders are the softest-kicking of all, in part because the gas system absorbs a certain amount of energy and in part because the mechanics are such that recoil is spread over a greater length of time.

Time is a crucial factor. The more slowly energy is expended, the less intense it feels. You could take an eight-pound bowling ball, place it on your foot, release it slowly and not feel much discomfort; but drop it on your foot from even a few inches' height, transferring all the energy at once, and it's a whole different matter. Though recoil from a gas-actuated autoloader lasts only a few milliseconds longer than from other types of gun, it's enough. We can't notice the difference in time, but we certainly can tell the difference in kick.

The angle at which a gun recoils also affects the way we perceive the kick. The ideal angle is straight backward, so all the energy is directed toward the shooter's shoulder and upper chest, which is the most massive part of our anatomy that's in contact with the gun. This is determined to some extent by the alignment of barrel and stock but more so by the configuration of the stock itself and the overall balance of the gun. A shot fired from the lower barrel of an over/under, for instance, sends the gun more nearly straight back than one from the upper tube, because the center of the lower bore is more closely lined up with the center of the butt. Even so, an over/under that's butt-heavy and muzzle-light tends to recoil upward rather than back, and being socked on the cheekbone by a gunstock does nothing to enhance either the pleasure of shooting or one's ability to hit anything.

A properly fitted stock is a great help in making a gun feel less kicky. If the comb is too high, you have to press your cheek hard against the wood in order to look down the rib, so any upward movement at all means a healthy whack. Too much drop is just as bad, because it promotes an even greater tendency for the butt to jump under recoil. American guns built around the turn of the century were typically made with two inches or more of drop at the comb, and those old dog-legs kick like the proverbial mule.

Stocks that are too short can kick badly as well, right to the point of driving your trigger-hand thumb into your nose as the gun comes back. A stock that's slightly too long is generally better than one too short, but if it's much too long, you'll mount it on your upper arm instead of your shoulder, which can be punishing.

The butt of the stock should be angled so its entire surface is in contact with your shoulder when the gun is pointing right where you're looking. If the angle is overly obtuse, the toe of the stock digs into your chest under recoil. If it's not obtuse enough, only the heel touches your shoulder, and that makes the gun want to slip and slide when you shoot it.

Even a perfectly tailored gun can kick like a demon if you handle it improperly. The trick is to stay balanced and loose so that your whole upper body—hands, arms, shoulder, chest, and back—takes the shock. A large, flexible mass can absorb recoil energy more comfortably than a small, rigid one.

With your body in balance, you can achieve maximum kick-resistance in several ways. Hold the gun in a firm grip (but not a stranglehold), especially with your leading hand. Keeping your leading hand well extended not only promotes the most accurate pointing but also allows your arm to absorb part of the recoil.

You might be surprised at how important a balanced body really is unless you take a shot sometime when you're way off balance. I was hunting ducks one time with a couple of chums, using a 16-bore L.C. Smith that was a dandy for shooting over decoys with a one-ounce upland load of No. 6. It was a pussycat for kick, or at least it was till some mallards surprised us and I fired from a crouch about halfway between sitting and standing, upon which Sweet Sixteen put me right on my butt in the bottom of the blind. My companions thought this was hugely funny.

To keep your body flexible, stand up straight, with your feet as close together as is comfortable. The contorted postures you often see at skeet and trap clubs do nothing for smooth gun handling nor dealing comfortably with recoil.

Neither does holding the gun tightly against your shoulder. In fact, that can make kick feel sharper because it concentrates the energy in one place instead of distributed among hands and arms.

The blast of a shot charge leaving the muzzle has no physical relationship to either recoil or kick, but it has both a physical and a psychological effect upon the shooter. As I discuss in a later chapter, gunfire assaults our ears intensely enough to do real and lasting damage to our hearing apparatus. The sensory shock is the equivalent of a physical blow, and that's exactly how we react to it. The blast makes the kick feel more intense. Attenuate the noise, and the sensation of kick is diminished as well. Wearing effective muffs or earplugs is crucial.

Although no one fully understands all the implications of how we react psychologically to kick, we do know that it has a cumulative effect, which is the phenomenon known as flinching. Flinching is complex, but in a nutshell, it's an acquired fear of shooting, brought on by repeated jolts of recoil and repeated exposure to muzzle-blast. Eventually, a shooter's brain and nervous system reaches something like critical mass and becomes reluctant to obey his will to pull a trigger. In an extreme case, he simply can't pull it to fire a shot and has to have a release trigger installed, which sets the sear when pulled and trips the sear when released.

A flinch-afflicted shooter is apt to do all sorts of weird things in anticipation of getting kicked—yank the gun sharply down with his leading hand, lift his cheek away from the stock, jerk his shoulders forward, even lurch forward a step or two. Sometimes he does these just as he pulls the trigger, sometimes just afterward, and sometimes he does them instead of pulling it. Target shooters are most liable to develop a flinch, simply because they fire more shots than game shooters do.

I have a notion that concentration is a factor in flinching. I know it's a factor in how we perceive recoil. The less focused on the target I am, the more I feel the kick. When I flinch, it's always while shooting skeet or clays, perhaps not paying as much attention as I could be, or field-testing a gun that may not fit me very well.

I'm most keenly aware of recoil when shooting at a patterning board. Then, when I'm thinking of nothing except hitting a four-foot sheet of steel, pulling the trigger, and getting kicked for it, even a 28-gauge is uncomfortable to shoot.

On the other hand, I seldom notice recoil at all when I'm shooting game, because nothing captures my concentration like a bird in the air. I'm only marginally aware of even the muzzle blast. No one is immune, however, and I have some very unfond

memories of shooting driven pheasants in England with a borrowed gun and some miserably overloaded Italian shells. I've
never taken such a pounding. By the last day, it was all I could
do to stay on the gun, and needless to say, I did not shoot especially well.

On the other hand, nothing has convinced me more that
the combination of a properly set up gun, reasonable cartridges,
and good earplugs can do wonders to tame the sensation of
kick than a certain day I spent shooting doves in Argentina a
couple of years ago.

The province of Córdoba is home to eared doves in pesti-
lential numbers, so many and so agriculturally destructive that
the government used to pay a bounty of one shotgun cartridge
for every pair of dove feet turned in. You can literally shoot as
much as you can stand. To that point, I'd never fired more than
about 300 shells in a single day at anything, but having the
right gun, the right cartridges, and the right opportunity all in
one place, I decided to see what shooting two cases—1,000
cartridges—would be like.

We set up in a place the guides call The Window, a vast area
of scrub-grown foothills. It's a roost for so many doves that the
first birds to leave in the morning are on their way back from
feeding while the late-sleepers are still heading out. If I hadn't
seen some other places like it in Argentina, I wouldn't have
believed my own eyes. There are birds in the air, lots of them,
every day from daylight to dark.

Our shells were good, one-ounce loads of sensible velocity,
about 1,200 feet per second. I had my AyA No. 2, a 6½-pound
12-bore I had built specifically for shooting in far-flung parts
of the world. It fits me as well as a gun can fit and sports one of
David Trevallion's lovely leather-covered Pachmayr Decelerator recoil pads. We've been just about everywhere together and
I love it to distraction, but never more than I did that day.

I shot a case of shells in the morning and another after
lunch. It wore me out, just from the continual acts of raising
the gun, firing, working the top lever, opening the gun and
reloading. My forearms ached like fire. The thumb of my right-

hand glove was in shreds from the checkering on the lever and safety button.

But kick never became a problem, not even toward the end, which surprised me. I expected my shoulder to be a collage of black and blue; finding that it wasn't surprised me even more. It was red from the abrasion of my shirt under the gun butt, but not bruised in the least. This I attribute to the Decelerator pad, which seems to have the perfect consistency for absorbing shock.

That the whole thing didn't turn into a grueling, painful ordeal I can only attribute to having all the right components. Had the gun not fit so well or had the loads been even slightly heavier, it might have worked out differently. I won't ever again shoot that much at one time, so I'll never know. I'm satisfied with having been there, done that, and lived to tell the tale. After all, a gun only needs to be lethal at one end.

Ounces to Grains Conversions

¾ ounce = 328.0 grains
⅞ ounce = 382.2 grains
1 ounce = 437.5 grains
1⅛ ounces = 492.1 grains
1¼ ounces = 546.7 grains

For converting other charge weights, ⅛ ounce equals 54.7 grains.

Velocities of Factory Loads

Gauge	Dram equivalent	Shot Charge (ounces)	Muzzle Velocity (feet per second)
12	3¼	1¼	1220
12	3¼	1⅛	1255
12	3¼	1	1290
12	3	1⅛	1200
12	2¾	1⅛	1145
12	2¾	1	1180
16	3	1⅛	1240
16	2¾	1⅛	1185
16	2¾	1	1220
16	2½	1	1165
20	2¾	1	1220
20	2½	1	1170
20	2½	⅞	1200
28	2½	¾	1295
28	2	¾	1200

Ordinary Load—60 Yards

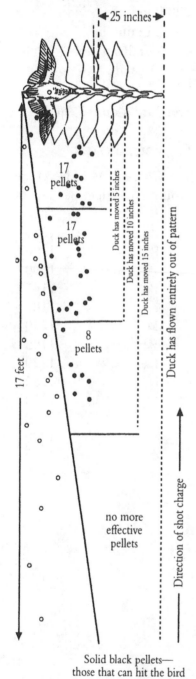

25 inches

17 pellets

17 pellets

8 pellets

Duck has moved 5 inches

Duck has moved 10 inches

Duck has moved 15 inches

Duck has flown entirely out of pattern

17 feet

no more effective pellets

Direction of shot charge

Solid black pellets—
those that can hit the bird

Super-X Load—60 Yards

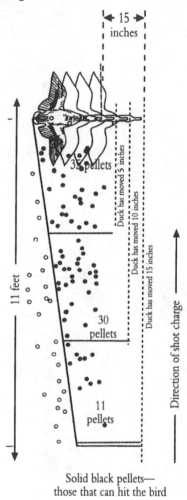

15 inches

35 pellets

30 pellets

11 pellets

Duck has moved 5 inches

Duck has moved 10 inches

Duck has moved 15 inches

11 feet

Direction of shot charge

Solid black pellets—
those that can hit the bird

7

SHOT
STRINGING

A swarm of shot begins expanding in diameter the moment it leaves the muzzle of a gun and continues expanding until the combined forces of atmospheric resistance and gravity bring the pellets to the ground. That's how shotguns work and why they exist.

Pellet spread determines the effectiveness of the gun and also its limitations. Over a certain distance the pellets remain close enough to one another that any object they encounter will be hit by several, and multiple strikes is what shatters clays and brings game birds to bag. Eventually, though, they spread too far apart relative to the size of the target, and the distance at which that happens is the limit of the gun's consistently effective range.

This much you can see on a patterning board. Just fire six or eight shots, starting at ten yards and backing up about five yards after each one, and compare the densities.

But there are a couple of things a patterning board can't show. One is that a swarm expands in a bell-shaped curve rather than the neat, straight-sided cone that's usually used to illustrate how a shotgun shoots; this is interesting but of no practical consequence.

Nor does the board show that shot travels from the gun to the target in a string, not as a flat, expanding disc. This is extremely important, because the length of the string is a key factor in the efficiency of any given load.

Time was, stringing was a chronic problem, though relatively few cared and even fewer realized how bad it was, because no one had any reliable means of measuring a shot string as it traveled through the air. But in the early 1920s, researchers at the Western Cartridge Company developed and patented an instrument they called the Flightometer, which could fix the position of every pellet in a swarm at any distance from the gun. From it they learned that the pellets from typical factory cartridges of the day strung out about twenty feet at normal shooting distances, and in some cases as much as thirty feet.

With that knowledge in hand, it was a simple matter to plot out the effect of both long and short shot strings and to see why the one is far less efficient than the other. The illustration on page 54, taken from a 1934 Western Cartridge pamphlet, accurately tells the tale. The longer the string, the sparser the pattern density at any point and the greater the possibility of a bird flying right through it virtually or literally unscathed.

Western Cartridge owner John Olin correctly surmised that stringing was principally caused by deformed pellets—those at the base of the shot column that got flattened by the initial thrust of gases from the powder and those that scraped against the barrel wall as they traveled down the bore. The pellets that managed to stay round flew true and fairly closely bunched while the deformed ones trailed along behind, rapidly losing velocity.

Olin's solution was to develop a progressive-burning powder, which more gradually accelerated the shot charge down the barrel rather than blasting it out of the case, and to use shot alloyed with antimony and plated with copper, which resisted deformation because it was considerably harder than pure lead. The result, Super-X shotshells, were the most efficient cartridges ever made to that point in history.

Other manufacturers eventually followed along similar lines, and shot strings by and large grew shorter. The potential for making them shorter yet came in the 1960s, with the introduction of polyethylene shot-cup wads that afford the shot charge maximum cushioning and protection while in the cartridge and the barrel.

It would be nice to say that the technology magically erased the long shot string from the gunning world, but it didn't. In fact, some of the loads you can buy right now string almost as badly as the ones great-granddad used before World War I, and some of the worst offenders are small-gauge rounds loaded with small shot, which means that the shell pockets they're most likely to end up in belong to upland hunters like you and me.

As with any problem, you have to know the cause before you can find the right solution, and while deformed pellets are still the main gremlins in stringing, there's more than one answer to how they get that way.

Size is a factor. Small pellets deform more easily than big ones, simply because the greater mass of large shot helps them keep their shape. It is therefore crucial that small shot be relatively harder, which means a higher percentage of antimony alloy which in turn means higher cost of manufacture and higher cost to the end user. It's an almost invariable rule that the cheaper the cartridge, the softer the shot inside it, and the softer the shot, the more it's going to string.

But even hard shot can string excessively, and nothing makes it do so more readily than cramming too much of it down a gunbarrel. To my mind, the size and weight of a shot charge in relation to bore diameter is the single most important factor, after hardness, in determining whether a shot string will be long or short.

The only way to get more pellets into a cartridge of any given gauge is to make the shot column longer. This means more shot on the outside of the column, and even the best shot cups do not offer absolute protection from damage against the barrel wall.

Then there's the matter of getting this long column moving in the first place. The heavier the charge, the more it resists moving, and the longer it is, the more surface area is on contact with the cartridge case and the bore, which increases friction. All this means that the pellets at the base of the column are subjected to more pressure and are more likely to deform and lag behind the rest of the swarm.

But even if you could somehow get every last one into the air still perfectly round, they're more strung-out to begin with than the shot in a shorter column. And they're pretty much going to stay strung out, especially fired through the open-choke barrels that uplanders need. There's good evidence to suggest that pellets fired through a full choke do actually close ranks a bit. Tightly bunched leading pellets in effect break a trail through the air, so those immediately behind encounter less resistance and can move slightly faster than the leaders.

But switching to full chokes isn't the answer. Stringing is a classic instance where prevention is better than any cure.

The key is to use very hard shot in the shortest reasonable column relative to bore size. That, more than anything else, promotes short strings. The shorter column contains fewer pellets than heavier loads, but at the same time, fewer of them get damaged by the initial thrust of gases and by contact with the barrel.

If you think about the loads in which long shot columns are confined in narrow bores, it's easy to guess which ones are the worst stringers: almost every three-inch 12 and 20, the one-ounce 28, and any .410, especially the three-inch .410, which is a little ballistic nightmare that no amount of technology will ever make into an efficient cartridge.

The best way to be sure of getting relatively short strings is to use target shells for game shooting. Target loads almost always contain the hardest shot and most highly protective wads. Among what's now available for skeet, trap, sporting clays, and flyer pigeons, you can find top-notch cartridges suitable for every upland bird.

But if you want the shortest strings of all and wonderfully comfortable cartridges that're deadly as lightning on game, use shot charges lighter than the nominal standard for the gauge ⅞-ounce 12s and ¾-ounce 20s. You can get the 12-bores as factory rounds from Estate and Fiocchi and the 20s from Estate.

The standard ¾-ounce 28-gauge is a short-stringing round to begin with, especially at target velocities. Any top-quality skeet or clays load is ideal. Don't fall victim to the old Magnum myth and start fretting about being undergunned. You won't be, I promise.

But if you still have any misgivings about their effectiveness, shoot a few boxes at targets before you take them to the field. What you'll find are cartridges that will reduce clay targets to puffs of smoke at any distance from which you'd take a reasonable crack at a quail, grouse, woodcock, or grainfield dove.

Lately I've been fooling with an Arrieta 12-gauge game gun bored for two-inch shells. The two-inch 12 is an old English invention that never became popular anywhere else, which is a pity because it's a lovely combination of light weight and astonishing ballistics. With 27-inch barrels, this Arrieta weighs two ounces under six pounds and is balanced to handle extremely well. But what's most remarkable is the performance of the cartridges in this case, English Lyalvales loaded with ¾-ounce of shot.

Now firing a 28-gauge load through a 12-bore gun may sound outrageous, but if you could see what it'll do to a clay target at any distance out to forty yards or more, you'd become an instant believer. Everyone who's tried it has. The clays don't just shatter; if they're well inside the pattern, they disappear in a cloud of dust. A bird would fare just the same.

What makes all these loads perform so efficiently is an exquisitely short shot string. Even though they carry relatively few pellets, a very high percentage of them reach the target and all pretty much at the same time. A shotgun can't get any deadlier than that.

The ill effects of shot stringing are most pronounced on a crossing target, least so on one that's going straight away, which means that the most maneuverable birds—doves, woodcock, and grouse—put a premium on short strings. But any game bird can present a shot where it's apt to fly right out of a strung-out swarm or, worse, get tagged with one or two pellets and become a fly-away cripple.

The less strung out your shot swarms are, the less likely you are to get strung out over missed or unrecovered game.

8

THE HUMBLE
REVOLUTION

In 1960, the Food and Drug Administration approved The Pill for sale in the United States, and Remington Arms introduced its SP-type shotshell. It's hard to say which had the greater impact on subsequent history, but there's no question that each represented the beginning of a new era.

The SP case was radically new, a polyethylene tube (the "P" part of the name) with a brass-plated steel head (the "S"), and it was many things that the standard paper case of the time was not: waterproof, swell-proof, immensely durable, and slick enough to feed smoothly through any repeating action.

It was quite an improvement, but the really revolutionary part was inside: a one-piece shot-cup wad, also of polyethylene. Remington called it the Power Piston, and along with similar items soon after devised by other manufacturers, it ushered in the modern age of the shotgun cartridge.

Complex, sophisticated systems often depend upon humble components. In practical terms, any gun is only as good as the ammunition it fires, and a cartridge is only as efficient as the wad inside it. Powder burns, releasing gas that drives the shot charge down the bore. The trick is to keep the gas behind the shot column, where it can generate maximum thrust and produce consistent velocities from one shell to the next. Something therefore has to seal the bore, keeping the gas column where it does the most good, and that's the wad's job.

And it's no easy job, because it amounts to juggling two essentially opposite requirements. The seal has to be good enough to resist high pressure—pressure enough to accelerate a roughly one-ounce mass from dead-still to a speed of 1,200 to 1,400 feet per second in a distance of less than two feet. But the seal also has to be movable, and readily so. If it isn't, the gas, adamant in its expansion, will simply blow open the barrel.

In the old, muzzleloading days, wads could be anything from a scrap of cloth or felt or leather to a crumpled-up cud of paper or even a handful of grass. And a shotgun needed two, one directly over the powder and another on top of the shot, to keep it from rolling out of the barrel. Over-enthusiastic use of the ramrod in seating a wad of some high-friction material often led to spectacular results.

By the time the muzzleloading gun reached the peak of perfection, wads typically were wafers of pasteboard, fiber, or felt punched out with a cutter and mallet, and these naturally were used in the earliest self-contained cartridges. In fact, such wads were used in shotshells for better than a hundred years, and you could still buy them for reloading as late as the 1970s; card, fiber, and felt of various thicknesses, some lubricated, some not. If I dug around my shop long enough I could probably still find a few Mould-Tite and Feltan-Bluestreak filler wads left over from thirty years ago. Combining two or three different sizes to build wad columns of proper height was time-consuming, and the thinner ones could tilt inside the case as you tried to seat them, but they worked. Which was good, because until about the mid-'60s they were all we had.

(Actually, felt and card wads are available even now, because black-powder shooters still use them, but they can be hard to find. If your local shops don't carry them, try Dixie Gunworks or Ballistic Products.)

Remington's Power Piston, followed shortly by Winchester's AA wad, Federal's Champion, the Alcan Unisleeve, and a few others, changed all that. At first, the factories used the more elaborate shot-cup versions only in their top-of-the-line target loads; for cheaper shells they devised various polyethylene over-powder wads—the Remington "H" wad, Winchester Universal Cup, Alcan Air-Wedge, and so on. They were all about equally good in forming a very efficient gas seal, and they were all designed according to the same principle—a hollow base with a relatively thin edge called the obturating skirt. This is the same principle that made the Minié bullet of Civil War days efficient. Gas in the hollow base expands the skirt so it presses against the barrel wall and prevents gas from escaping past it.

As an additional advantage, polyethylene is considerably slicker than felt or fiber and therefore sets up less friction against either the cartridge case or the bore. Velocities became higher and more consistent and chamber pressures lower.

And while the obturating-skirt base greatly improved the shotshell's interior ballistics, the polyethylene wad's shot cup and cushioning posts did even better things for exterior ballistics, just by keeping a higher percentage of the shot pellets nice and round.

A round object has a poor aerodynamic shape to begin with. Unlike a pointed bullet, even a perfect sphere plows along through the air, building enormous atmospheric resistance, rapidly shedding velocity and energy; for an imperfect sphere, the effect is even worse, and the projectile becomes highly erratic besides, spinning wildly off-course. Clearly, the more shot pellets that leave the muzzle as nearly round as they started, the more of them are able to contribute something useful to pattern density and striking power.

Pellets get brutalized inside a gun barrel. The initial thrust of gas, which drives the shot column out of the case, starts the bottom of the column moving first, so those pellets get crushed against the ones farther up. Then all the pellets on the outside of the column scrape against the barrel wall as the column goes ramming down the bore. Lead being softer than steel, it's easy to imagine what happens; once the swarm gets out of the muzzle, the pellets on the edge, having suddenly become half-spheres, go looping off as flyers while those in the rear lag behind, stringing out as much as twenty feet or more.

About all the cartridge makers could do was use progressive-burning powders that accelerate the shot charge more gradually than black or the old bulk-smokeless propellants; alloy the shot with antimony to make it relatively hard; and build up a fairly thick column of felt and fiber wads for cushioning. All gunmakers could do was polish their bores to reduce friction as much as possible. It was less than ideal, but there it was. Shotgun cartridges just weren't all that efficient which, incidentally, is why choke-boring was invented.

The polyethylene wad changed that, too. Nearly all the shot-cup versions have a section between base and cup that is more or less collapsible, meant to compress under the initial thrust of gas and absorb some of the shock before it reaches the pellets, which means the pellets in the bottom of the charge don't get as badly crushed.

But the shot cup itself is the real key to improved efficiency, because it forms a buffer between pellets and bore and keeps the whole outer layer from being so badly damaged. In the 1960s and '70s, ammunition companies often used separate plastic collars in their less-expensive shells (and some still do), but they're only marginally effective because they're too thin to do much real buffering. But the best shot-cup wads, the ones with the thickest cup walls, truly do the trick. They don't protect every pellet, neither through the cup nor the collapsible sections, and they don't eliminate the need for hard shot, but they certainly make shotshells more efficient than ever before.

Patterns instantly became about 10 percent denser, which meant that barrels bored for old-style cartridges shot tighter by one standard increment of choke. With the new shells, improved-cylinder barrels essentially became modified, modified became full, and full became really full. (In fact, it's my opinion that the shot-cup wad has now made the whole concept of choke virtually obsolete, but that's a can of worms we'll open some other time.)

Combined with cartridge cases also made of polyethylene, the plastic wads were a revolution, and in the span of just a few years during the '60s, they transformed American shotshells from good to the world's best.

Which is not to say that a shot-cup wad is a universal prescription. Handloaders especially still need to be careful about properly matching wads and cases. Some plastic cases, like Winchester AAs and Remington RXPs, have tapered walls, so the inside diameter is slightly smaller at the base than at the mouth; others are straight-walled. Wads designed for tapered cases typically have slightly shorter obturating skirts, and these don't work quite as efficiently in straight-walled cases.

Actually, in some instances they don't work at all. Years ago, I did my old friend Spence a favor and loaded a few boxes of 20-bores for him in anticipation of the quail season. I don't remember the exact recipe, but it was in a published loading manual and called for, let's say, a Remington wad in a Federal Hi-Power case and a light charge of fine-grained powder, like PB.

They worked fine on our first couple of hunts, but then one of them came up a squib, a little popper that just barely pushed the wad to the end of the barrel. In handloading parlance, those can usually be filed under Forgetting the Powder Charge. It's a bit embarrassing and can be dangerous if you don't check the bore and, if necessary, push the wad out with a stick.

A half-hour later he had another one, and then another, both of which required a broken-off ragweed stem to dislodge the wads. And then it got really ugly. I'd hear Spence thrashing around in the brush, the sound of birds taking off, and *poonk-poonk* from his gun, followed by very coarse language in litanies that grew progressively longer, louder, and less complimentary toward my parents in their implications.

I was utterly mystified. Like every handloader, I've been known to miss a powder charge now and then, but not ten in the same box. Finally I asked him for one of the shells and split it open with my pocketknife. The powder wasn't missing at all; it was in the center of the wad, neatly packed around the cushioning posts. As that's not where I put it, I was even more mystified until I figured out that the base of the wad was just a tad too small for the base of the case and that a few hours of jiggling in Spence's pocket had caused the tiny grains of powder to migrate around the wad base and into the open center, where it was effectively beyond reach of the primer flash.

It was a good lesson. For one thing it proved that even though certain components can be combined safely, the result won't necessarily be efficient. It also points out a certain wisdom in using wads and cases from the same manufacturer or at least matching those of the same basic configuration.

And it suggests that there are no extraneous or unimportant components of either guns or cartridges, which is a lesson on the order of Ben Franklin's adage that begins "For want of a nail..." Or, in terms perhaps more relevant to the shooting world: If it's not one damn thing, it's sure to be something else.

9

AVOIRDUPOIS

Shotgunning is rife with pre-scriptions: An upland gun should have 26-inch barrels; smallbores are best for small game; wildfowl guns need to be long and heavy and tightly choked; you can't kill pheasants with anything less than a magnum load; on and on. Think about it for a few minutes, and you can make up your own list. The shooting world is full of them.

It's also full of baloney, and nowhere more conspicuously than in the prescriptions insisting that every gauge has its "best" range of overall weight and that "proper" balance can be determined with regard to nothing other than the gun itself.

You won't have to look far to find somebody who's willing to declare that a 16-bore ought to weigh from six to 6½ pounds or that 5¼ to 5¾ pounds is perfect for a 28, nor will you have much difficulty finding someone who's willing to believe it. The problem, as with most prescriptions in gundom, is that none of this takes account of the fact that in order to do what it's meant to do, a shotgun requires a shooter and that not all shooters are alike.

Handling characteristics aside for the moment, gross weight can be boon or bane, depending. If you're going to shoot targets or live pigeons, and therefore fire a substantial number of shots over a relatively short time, you'll eventually come to appreciate an extra pound or two, just for damping recoil a bit. If you're a quail or grouse hunter, on the other hand, and use your feet more than your trigger finger, those additional pounds have a way of increasing exponentially with the passage of time and distance from your vehicle. As a rule of thumb, target guns are more useful if they're relatively heavy and game guns are more comfortable if they're relatively light.

I say "relatively" advisedly, because gun weight is nothing if not relative. To a guy who stands six-foot-four and can bench-press a Volvo, a nine-pound gun is a mere feather. To my wife, who stands five-foot-one and has never weighed a hundred pounds, a six-pound gun is a burden. I'm somewhere between, and though I find the eight pounds' heft of my favorite target gun perfect for a clays course, I sure as hell don't want to carry it all day nor would expect to shoot it well if I did. To my taste, 6½ pounds of game gun is the max.

Actually, few upland hunters seem to handicap themselves by choosing guns that are too heavy, and those who do don't hang onto those guns for very long. This is good. As a combination of ballet and rodeo usually performed when one is off-balance, tangled up in something, or otherwise out of kilter, bird shooting is tough enough without trying to swing a piece that's ponderous as a bridge timber.

Unfortunately, though, a lot of hunters go too far the other way and opt for ultralights, and this is usually not good. Too little gross weight in a gun is just as bad as too much, possibly even worse. A big, heavy gun may be difficult to get moving after a bird with departure on its mind, but at least it tends to keep moving once you get it started, and a moving gun is a key factor in making things fall out of the sky.

I cringe inside every time I see a hunter uncase some wispy, short-nosed little thing, because I know exactly what's going to happen. It may be no more burdensome to carry around the woods or the fields than a pocketknife, but it's also not much more useful for a hunter of average size who wants to shoot consistently well.

Here's the problem: Very light guns are quick as whips to get started, but they're just as quick to stop. Every time you take your eyes off a moving target and look at the gun, the gun slows down. Our eyes are wonderful instruments, but they can't focus in two planes at once, and our hands naturally, unconsciously, do our eyes' bidding. Keep your eyes on a moving target and your hands will track it with a gun; look at the gun and your hands have no independently moving object to follow, so they stop. If the gun they're holding is heavy enough to create some momentum, the gun itself can help overcome the hesitation, but if it's so light that it has to be steered and pushed and guided every inch of the way, all it takes is one glance from target to gun and the bloody thing stops dead.

Even if you do keep your eyes on the target, you'll find that accurately tracing its flight line is more difficult with a very light gun. Too much weight in your leading hand makes a gun feel sluggish and unresponsive; too little weight fouls up your sense of accurate pointing.

How much is too much and how little is too little depends entirely upon the shooter. There are no prescriptions, no objective standards that truly apply. The best gun is not the lightest one you can find; it's the lightest one you can shoot. Finding your optimal weight range is a matter of experience and experiment. The more different guns you shoot, the better sense you'll have of what suits you best.

And once you find your best weight, stick with it; depart from it too radically and you're buying a first-class ticket to frustration. As I mentioned earlier, I do my best game shooting with guns of six to 6½ pounds. I can do okay with one that's a wee bit heavier, but with anything less my already-meager skill starts to come apart in a hurry. When I ordered a 28-gauge from Arrieta a few years ago I stipulated that under no circumstances was it to weigh less than six pounds. Conventional wisdom would throw up its hands in horror at that, arguing that a 28 can be much lighter with the implication that because it can be it therefore should be.

Well, of course it can be, but if it was, I couldn't shoot it worth a damn, and after all, I didn't order it as a means of making myself miserable. In the end, it came out at six pounds on the dot, I shoot it as well as I can shoot anything, and I love it to distraction. I feel the same way about my Fox 20 and my 12-bores by AyA and John Wilkes, the lightest of which weighs 6¼ pounds and the heaviest 6½.

Because all of my game guns are about the same weight, I can use any of them without having to adjust my muscles and mind to something unfamiliar. But they're also balanced the same way, and that's the real key.

Matching the gross weight of a gun to the shooter is important; matching the distribution of that weight to the way he handles it is crucial. In fact, I'd argue that apart from stock fit and trigger pull, balance is the single most important factor in determining how consistently well anyone can shoot any given gun.

The classic prescription has it that a gun should balance between the shooter's hands, and this is typically thought of as being right on the hinge pin of the action. But like other such dicta, it fails to account for the shooter as an individual.

One hand is always near the trigger, but there's considerable variance in where the other grips the barrels or fore-end. Some shooters feel most comfortable holding their guns close to the action; others take a longer hold, extending the leading hand almost as far as they can reach. Consequently, "between the hands" represents different actual balance points for different people.

Moreover, balancing a gun on its hinge pin may be cool in some theoretical way, but in practical terms it's useless because it not only fails to account for the shooter but also for the gun itself. Some guns have longer action bars than others, but any experienced shooter will tend to take the same hold with his forward hand, regardless of the gun. That's why stockmakers work to a balance point measured from the breech face and don't worry about where the hinge pin happens to be.

Now suppose you do achieve a balance that puts equal portions of a gun's total weight in either hand; will that make it feel just perfect? There's no way I can say what's going to feel best or swing most effectively for you, but I can tell you that none of my guns balance exactly between my hands, and I've had them set up that way on purpose.

Think back to what I suggested a while ago, about putting enough weight into your leading hand to promote a smooth, controllable swing. I've found that most game guns, especially relatively light ones, tend to feel twitchy with half the weight in my leading hand, but when slightly more than half the weight's out front they become eminently controllable. It doesn't interfere with quickness, but it does make them swing smoothly, helps me track flight lines as precisely as I'm capable of doing, and promotes just enough momentum to pull the muzzles through a target or a bird even if I commit a minor clutch or bobble. No gun can shoot itself, but I'm convinced that mine give me a substantial number of hits every year that would be misses if the guns were balanced differently.

You can experiment with this yourself, and I particularly recommend that you do if you have a gun that's lighter in the barrels than in the stock. All you have to do is tape some lead to the barrels—adding about an ounce at a time is usually enough—while you shoot some clays or a few rounds of skeet. You can scrounge up some old wheel-weights at any tire shop. It shouldn't take long to notice a difference in how your gun swings, and once you find what feels best, leave the weights in place and send it off to a gunsmith or stockmaker to be rebalanced.

With a double gun, he'll do it by boring wood out of the butt. Repeaters can often be rebalanced by replacing the wooden magazine plug with one made of metal, but if you shoot a pump gun or autoloader the chances are that it already has a slightly weight-forward feel. It makes double-gun purists cringe, but the fact is, you'll be hard-pressed to find a gun with more sheer pointability than a repeater right out of the factory box. That's why I'd bet nickels to doughnuts that the best wingshot you knew when you were a kid shot a Model 12.

Two things to remember. One is that nobody can tell you what feels best to you; a good stock fitter can prescribe proper dimensions, but you're the only one who knows exactly how your gun feels to you. The other is that every gun can be rebalanced. If you're a big guy you may need to trade off your ultralight for something that's more your size, but you'd be surprised at how much difference a balance job can make in even a gun that's too light for you to begin with.

It can go a long way toward making a swizzle-stick piece feel like a real gun, and if the art of wingshooting isn't at least half feel, then I haven't learned nearly as much as I think I have from forty years of fooling around with guns.

LEGEND

10

BESPEAKING A
BESPOKEN GUN

My friend Ben looked up
from the litter of catalogues, forms, notes, drawings, and lists
spread on the table and reached for his beer.

"Having fun sure can get complicated," he said, taking a
swig and ignoring the hummingbirds zooming under the patio
arbor on their fifth or sixth strafing run of the past hour. That's
where the feeders are, and they take it as their turf.

Fun can indeed get complicated, but name a better pastime
for a sunny May afternoon than working up the specs for a
new, custom-built gun.

Like a good many of my contemporaries, Ben has reached
an age where his level of disposable income can accommodate
the longtime dream of owning a bespoken gun, and like several
of my friends, he asked for my help in working his way through
the surprisingly complex paradigm of decisions that go along
with having a gun made to order.

Most are surprised by the number of choices to be made, which in itself is not surprising. For most of us, buying guns has always meant getting a new one straight from some dealer's inventory or a used one off the rack and taking it as it comes. We might have it altered later with a stock or choke job, but for the most part it's been a matter of What You See is What You Get. Deciding what to get before you ever see it is a different ballgame altogether.

Regardless of who's going to build your gun or how much you're going to pay for it, the ordering process is the same, and it begins with some basic decisions as to type, gauge, and the purposes your new gun will be meant to serve. Because the gun will be just what you ask for, you have to start by deciding what to ask.

Connecticut Shotgun is the only American factory that builds guns to order, so if you're not buying an A.H. Fox or a Galazan over/under, you'll be dealing with a foreign maker, either directly or through an American agent. That won't change the process, but it might make a difference in how best to place the order. More on this in a moment. The key point right now is that if you don't speak the maker's language and he doesn't speak yours, you're going to need an interpreter and it should be someone who knows guns and the lingo of guns in both languages. Working with an American agent can save a lot of confusion.

(Stuff can happen even when there isn't a language difference, as in the possibly apocryphal story of the Texan who ordered a gun from London. Finalizing the details over the phone, the salesman asked what sort of engraving he wanted, to which the Texan replied, "Aw, just some scrolls." Thanks to his accent and a less-than-pindrop phone connection, his gun arrived decorated with the engraved images of squirrels.)

Within limits, you'll have some latitude in specifying the gun's overall weight, and if you're an experienced shot you should have a good idea of what suits you best. Forget any nonsense you might hear about "proper" weight ranges diminishing as the gauge gets smaller. It's true that most smallbores weigh less than larger ones, but there's a point at which practicality should take precedence over theory. If you're a big or even average guy, chances are you don't shoot very well with a gun that weighs much less than six pounds, regardless of what gauge it is, so don't make the mistake of ordering a 5¼-pound 28-gauge just because somebody says that's what a 28 "ought" to weigh. I ordered mine at six pounds, and nobody who's handled it has ever thought it was too heavy.

Some Spanish makers build guns in two basic weights; for instance, a light 12-bore at about 6½ pounds and a heavy one at about 7½. With other makers you can specify exact weights. The important thing is that the weight needs to suit your physique. Remember, too, that wood density varies, so don't nitpick if the gun comes out an ounce or two more or less.

You can also specify the balance point, which is typically measured from the face of the standing breech. If you don't know what to ask for, find a gun with a balance you like, hang it in a loop of stout cord, move it back and forth till it lies level, and measure the distance from the string to the breech face.

Unless you already know what stock dimensions suit you, you'll need the services of a competent gun fitter, and it's a good idea to have the fitting done with the same sort of gun you plan to order. Applying to a side-by-side the dimensions taken from an over/under try-gun, or vice versa, won't give you the best results. Find out how the maker customarily expresses measurements, inches or millimeters, and have the fitter prescribe dimensions in the appropriate system. Ask, too, if you should express the dimensions of stock pitch in degrees, as some Italian makers prefer, or in actual lengths from the trigger to the heel and toe of the butt. All this is to make certain you and the maker are singing the same song, a bit of extra insurance that your gun will be just what you ask for.

Barrel length is your choice, and here, too, you should learn whether the maker is accustomed to working in inches or centimeters. With some it doesn't matter, but as virtually all the European trades except the British use the metric system, you might want to convert your wishes and express them that way.

Same with chamber length and choke constrictions. Standard European chambers are 65mm, 70mm, and 75mm, which correspond to 2½, 2¾, and 3 inches, respectively. Converting thousandth-inch choke dimensions to millimeters may be rather tricky, and depending upon the maker, you may not need to but it's always a good idea to specify chokes in actual measurements rather than simply asking for "improved cylinder" or "modified," designations that mean different things to different makers.

If you intend shooting steel shot in your new gun, be sure to tell the maker so he can leave the barrels appropriately thick. Some offer chrome-lined bores as an option but it's largely useless except to prevent corrosion, and it makes altering chokes very difficult.

You'll also need to decide on the rib style. For a side-by-side it can be the standard game rib, which is hollow and swamped; a flat rib, which will be file-matted on top; or a Churchill rib, which is slightly tapered from breech to muzzle and also tapers up the sides to a very narrow top. For an over/under you'll have the option of a solid or vent rib, either tapered or parallel.

If you get a gun from Purdey's or from one of the English makers who builds Purdey-type actions—Watson Brothers or Peter Nelson, for instance—your gun will intrinsically be a self-opener. From Holland & Holland, or virtually any other European maker, the self-opening feature is optional, and it's almost certain to be made on the Holland & Holland system. The choice of a self-opener is partly practical (it's handy for doves and driven game) and partly a matter of how far you care to go in adding bells and whistles.

For a side-by-side you can choose an action style—standard or round-body. Which you like is solely a matter of taste, but be aware that your choice will carry some implications for the rest of the gun. The stock of a round-body, for instance, will be rounded, too, without sharply defined lock edges or drop points.

There are essentially two ways to go about selecting wood. One is to visit the maker and pick the blank you like best, which is great fun, though I warn you, trying to choose one blank from an inventory of gorgeous walnut can lead to sensory overload.

Every stock blank is different, of course, but wood can be grouped according to the type of figure it has, and most of us have a preference for one sort or another. I want mine to be streaky with good contrast, you might like a lot of fiddleback, while someone else digs crotch-type sunburst or burl. If it's inconvenient to go to choose a specific blank, you can still specify the category. Find a photo of a stock you like, say in a magazine or auction catalogue, send it to the maker, and ask him to use a blank of similar type. I've done this a couple of times, and it's worked out extremely well.

Besides the dimensions, you have some other options regarding the stock. You can specify a splinter fore-end, semi- or full beavertail, a straight hand, half-hand, full pistol-grip, a palm-swell, a diamond hand, whatever you like. You can have a plain checkered butt, a buttplate, plain or leather-covered recoil pad, steel heel and toe pieces, or skeleton steel plate. You can have a gold or silver stock oval installed.

If you want to check the stock dimensions while the gun is in progress, you can make arrangements to visit the maker and test-fire it once it's been stocked. This shouldn't really be necessary, assuming you gave him the right numbers to begin with, but it can be done.

Double triggers are traditional for side-by-side guns, but nearly every maker offers a single as an option; with over/unders it's usually the other way around, though in some cases double triggers may not be available at all. If you're thinking about a single trigger for a side-by, think carefully. Some are excellent, some aren't, and those that aren't can be the source of endless problems. Much as I admire Spanish guns, I don't have much confidence in Spanish single triggers.

Regardless of which way you go, you can specify the weight of trigger pulls, either in pounds or kilograms. The rule of thumb is that the first sear should be set at half the weight of the gun and the second a half-pound more to guard against jar-off, though you might want them a wee bit heavier for a game gun. All of mine weigh from six and 6½ pounds, and the triggers are adjusted at 3½ and four pounds.

Then there's the matter of decoration. Nearly every maker has standard engraving patterns that you can choose among, or you can design your own. Every gun trade has its share of masters who can do anything you want by way of engraving and inlay, especially in Italy, where gun engraving has become something of a national art.

The bottom line is that there is no bottom line; you can have anything from your high-school graduation portrait or a picture of your goldfish to a map of your hometown or an erotic episode put on your gun so long as you're willing to pay the price. And it can be pricey. You can spend as much or more than the cost of the gun on decoration alone.

This is one area where you can let your wishes run wild, bound only by the heft of your checkbook. You can even specify the engraver himself (or herself) but if you do you'd better be young and patient, because all the big-name artisans are booked solid well into the next century.

Even if you take the path of least delay, it'll be a while before your gun is finished, anywhere from several months to a couple of years or more. The maker will give you an estimate up front, and in return you should give him some slack and not bug him if it takes a bit longer. The point, after all, is to have a gun built to whatever level of refinement is appropriate to the price you pay, not turn the project into a race against the calendar.

Besides, the anticipation is part of the pleasure, knowing that someday, late or soon, you'll end up with a gun that was built just for you. From the moment you first put it together and swing on the bird that's flying through your mind, it'll all seem worthwhile: the expense, the time, and the sweet complexities of having fun.

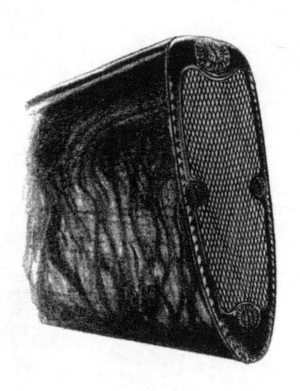

11

BUTTPLATES
& PADS

In the beginning, hand-held firearms were little more than barrels fastened to wooden poles. In about the fourteenth century, someone decided that handling and accuracy could be improved by mounting the barrel on a wooden beam that a gunner could rest on top of his shoulder. After another hundred-odd years, someone else came up with the notion of shaping the beam in such a way that it could be held against the shoulder. Enter the gunstock as we know it.

Setting aside variations in style and taste, the concept of the stock has changed scarcely at all in the past 500 years and neither has the matter of deciding what to do about the rear end of it. One writer a few years back referred to this as "butt treatment" which sounds at best like the sort of silly euphemism that describes ties as "neckwear" and at worst like a proctological procedure, but there it is.

And there, more to the point, is the butt-end of a stock, begging to be finished off in some neat, possibly even practical way. The choices now are virtually no different from those that existed a half-millennium past.

The traditional English approach is simply to round off the wood, smooth it down, and dress up the surface with a patch of checkering. The European trades that have adopted the English style—which is to say, most of them—do this as well. It makes for a neat, understated appearance but offers no protection to the wood. With a plain, checkered butt, the point of the toe is especially liable to chip or split from an accidental blow.

Some stockmakers solve this problem with heel and toe pieces, small steel plates inletted to the rear surface of the butt at top and bottom. They protect the stock and, engraved and blued or color-hardened, lend a decidedly handsome look as well.

The so-called skeleton butt is a steel plate with the center cut out. This protects the edges of the butt as well as the heel and toe while leaving a sizeable area for checkering. To some eyes, a skeleton is the most elegant treatment of all. Nearly all of the old American makers offered it as an option, although relatively few customers chose it, and those who did usually ordered it on higher-grade guns. Among shooters and collectors who fancy American guns, finding a Fox or Parker with an original skeleton butt is a real coup. I don't recall ever seeing it mentioned in L.C. Smith catalogues, but I wouldn't be surprised if a few Smith guns were made that way.

More recently, a skeleton butt was standard fare for Parker Reproductions, although they weren't installed the traditional way, which is to inlet the plate all around. Instead, Parker Repro skeletons were given a separate wood insert, and the whole assembly fits on like a solid buttplate. It was a clever way of reducing handwork in the factory without altering the appearance.

Connecticut Shotgun currently offers a skeleton butt as an option for new Fox guns. So far as I know, it's the only full-scale American maker to do so. Any good stockmaker can install one as a custom job, of course, but it won't be cheap; inletting a skeleton is a tedious, painstaking job. Even the simpler heel and toe pieces require several hours each to file up and fit properly.

Perhaps the most widely used approach is to cover the entire surface of the butt with a plate held in place by a couple of screws. These have been made of everything from iron to ivory, buffalo horn to exotic woods, but for the past hundred years, hard rubber, Bakelite, and various other plastics have been the materials of choice.

A buttplate or heelplate, as the English call it, is the perfect solution for high-volume factory production. It's inexpensive, easy to fit, and looks good. If a stock is bored out to adjust the balance of a gun, a plate covers the holes that would have to be plugged if the butt was to be checkered. It also covers the hole in a stock attached by a drawbolt, and that one has to remain open.

Virtually every American gunmaker installed a buttplate as standard equipment. Most have been rather plain—smooth at heel and toe and grooved in the center—but some are quite distinctively decorated. Parker's famous "dogs-head" logo is a good example. So is Winchester's old stylized monogram and the simple elegance of some Browning designs.

Buttplates, checkered butts, heel and toe pieces, and skeletons all share two characteristics: They don't keep a stock from sliding, neither on your shoulder nor on a smooth floor if you prop a gun against a wall or the side of a duck blind, and they do not absorb recoil. Neither of these is necessarily a disadvantage.

A gun that properly fits the shooter isn't much prone to slipping off the shoulder when fired, and being careful about where you place a gun when you put it down is only common sense. Moreover, recoil isn't necessarily an issue except when you're shooting stiff loads or firing a great many shots over short periods of time.

But none of that means there aren't benefits in pads. Some have to do with recoil, others don't.

Attaching some sort of cushion to a gun butt is a practice no doubt as old as firearms themselves, but the modern era of recoil pads began just over a hundred years ago. In England, Walter Scott of Birmingham patented an India-rubber pad in 1871; Hugh Silver of London patented a rubber pad in 1874 and a refined version in 1886. Cheltenham gunmaker Edwinson Green patented a similar device in 1885. Of them all, Silver's became, and remains, the most famous.

John Onderdonk of Philadelphia invented one of the earliest pads patented in the U.S.—air-filled and vented so it could compress and reinflate. In the same 1884 patent, Onderdonk described a spring-loaded buttplate that served to absorb recoil, but a Pittsburgh man, William Miller, had beat him to it with an 1875 patent for a similar idea.

A vast variety of more conventional rubber pads have been produced since the turn of the century by Jostam, Hawkins, Noshoc, Fray-Mershon, Pachmayr, and others. At present, Galazan's of New Britain, Connecticut, manufactures a good selection, including exact replicas of old-style Silver's, Hawkins, and Winchester pads. (Galazan also makes replicas of classic American buttplates—Parker, Fox, Remington, L.C. Smith, Winchester, and others.)

Since the beginning, the recoil-absorbing capacity of pads has varied. Most of the old Silver's jobbies, for instance, tend to be hard as bricks, certainly handsome, in their rich, orangy red, but not much help for kick. Even now, some pads are softer than others. Of the ones I've tried, Pachmayr's Decelerator and Galazan's Technically Superior Pad seem to me the best at damping recoil.

Even when recoil isn't a problem, a pad is an excellent way to lengthen a stock that's too short. Pads typically are ⅞ to one inch thick, but you can get them up to 1½ inches. For even more extension, you can get spacers that match the plastic base of certain pads.

Depending on what they're made of, some pads have a slightly tacky surface that helps keep the gun from slipping on your shoulder when you fire the first shot. You can get the same effect by gluing a patch of thin, soft leather onto the face of the pad. This seems to work especially well if there's also a leather shoulder patch on your shooting jacket or vest.

Leather-faced pads add something to a gun's appearance as well, but the handsomest of all, to my eye, is one that's completely covered in leather. Leather-covered pads are elegant, wonderfully comfortable, and if the leather is top quality, remarkably durable. David Trevallion made one for my 12-bore AyA that's stood up to seven years of shooting and about 70,000 cartridges. It's showing a bit of wear at the edges, but so am I and for that matter, so's Trevallion. Truth to tell, the pad probably still looks better than either of us.

Any pad needs to be installed by someone who knows his work. The standard method is to screw it on and then grind it to size using a power sander followed by chisels and files; the craftsmanship lies in getting everything fitted and squared up to a gnat's whisker without nicking the stock, which is a lot more difficult to do than it is to describe.

A leather-covered pad is trickier still. It needs to be ground .020- to .025-inch undersized to accommodate the thickness of the leather; plugs need to be cut to fill the screw holes; and the leather needs to be put on so it lies perfectly smooth all around, without any creases or wrinkles. This is especially tricky where it goes under the toe. It's also tricky to get a tight, smooth fit on a very soft pad without distorting the shape.

Almost any sort of leather will work so long as it's skived thinly enough, but pigskin is traditional in England and goatskin is widely used in Europe. Goatskin finishes to a smooth, shiny surface that some shooters like; pigskin is a bit rougher and grips a shooting jacket extremely well.

From a first-rate craftsman, a leather-covered pad will cost $350 to $400, more if the stock has to be plugged and redrilled or bridged to accommodate the new screws. I suppose you could have one made for less, but as with everything else, you get what you pay for. I'm reasonably handy at tying flies, checkering stocks, making cases, and other such painstaking work, and I've tried covering a pad or two, just to see if I could do it.

I can, but if you saw them, you'd think they were overpriced at ten bucks; watch a real craftsman do it, examine the results as closely as you want, and $400 will look like a bargain.

And that's the story—except that having laid down nearly 1,700 words without so much as one feeble pun in a subject that simply begs for it just doesn't feel right. So let me say that regardless of whether you prefer plain checkered wood, heel and toe pieces, a skeleton, plate, or pad...nothing is quite so appealing as a really attractive butt.

12

OUT OF SIGHT, OUT OF MIND

Some things you just have to wonder about. Like the signs you sometimes see on the doors of buildings, the ones that read "No Dogs Allowed Except Seeing-Eye Dogs." Who are those for?? Or like sights on shotguns in which case the question isn't *who?* but rather *why?*

I suppose the simplest answer is that firearms have always had some sort of front sight. You'll find them on flintlocks, wheellocks, matchlocks, all the way back to the beginning. Before rifling was invented, around the turn of the sixteenth century, all firearms were capable of firing both ball and shot, so a front sight on a gun from that era makes some sense. But even after guns were made specifically for shot, they still had sights. If you have the chance to visit a museum that has a good historical arms collection, check out the blunderbusses—short-barreled pieces with flared muzzles meant to scatter a shot charge over the widest possible area at very short range. Likely as not, you'll see a tiny little bead near the muzzle. That'll really make you wonder.

And of course, guns have sights to this day, usually simple beads, seldom larger than an eighth inch in diameter, made of steel, brass, ivory, or plastic. Some guns have a mid-bead, about half the size of the front one, placed roughly halfway between the muzzle and the breech.

Simple enough, but over the years, a few innovative types have decided that the bead could be improved upon. Bob N'chols, who was firearms editor of *Field & Stream* in the 1930s and '40s, invented a front sight he called the Bev-L-Blok; it was a little ramp-type steel block with a long, sloping end facing the shooter and a white plastic bead mounted on the slant. Poly-Choke later adopted it as part of the Poly variable-choke device. The Bradley sight also used a sizeable white bead but without the elevating ramp. From the shooter's point of view, it just looks like a bead sitting on the barrel or rib.

For years, Ithaca guns were fitted with what the company called the Raybar front sight, a fluorescent red plastic bar about half an inch long. Simmons made a similar item called the Glow Worm. And there was also the Trius Bi-Ocular, which showed a spot of light in its center, provided the shooter was looking down the barrel with his master eye. You can still find new guns that come with fluorescent plastic front sights, and they look to me just as garish as ever, about like hanging fuzzy dice from the rearview mirror of a Bentley.

Others have taken even wilder swings and invented gizmos meant to give the appearance of projecting a spot of light at the target. Weaver made a shotgun scope in the 1930s, a 1X affair meant to offer a wide field of view rather than magnification, but as the naked eye has an even wider field, I've never understood the point. Some others experimented with peep-type rear sights. And not surprisingly, yet others came up with attachments purporting to automatically establish the correct amount of forward allowance for crossing targets—gadgets with circular or rectangular frames that stuck out on either side of the muzzle. Theoretically, when you placed the target inside

one of the frames, depending on which way it was flying, of course, you had the right lead.

All these doodads were advertised with the implication that they could instantly turn the most fumblesome duffer into a deadly shot, and a few claimed the added advantage of "preventing cross-firing." "Cross-firing" is an old term for cross-dominance, which is the phenomenon of one's master hand and master eye being on opposite sides of the body. Yessir, friends and neighbors, Doctor Snakeoil's Magic Elixir is a sovereign remedy for lumbago, gout, brain fever, fallen arches, halitosis, and all manner of female complaints and two doses is guaranteed to grow hair on a watermelon...

Now, this is not to say there's no practical reason to have some sort of sight on a gun. Any rib on a barrel, or between two barrels, is a sight inasmuch as it helps the shooter bring the barrel in line with his eye. More important, a properly fitted stock is also a form of sight, because it makes a gun shoot right where you're looking without having to do anything but lift it to your cheek. There's even a good reason to have a center bead on a trap, skeet, or pigeon gun; in all three games you're allowed to mount the gun before you call for the target, and getting set up so that the front bead is right on top of the middle one, forming a figure-8, is a good way of obtaining exactly the same relationship between yourself and the gun every time. This is especially useful at trap, because the game requires an almost riflelike precision in dealing with a limited variety of angles.

Using sights as a reference in premounting a gun is about the extent of their usefulness. You don't aim a shotgun, you simply point it, and the one thing you never want to do when a target's in the air is look at the gun. When your eyes are focused sharply on the target, you still see the barrels, rib, and perhaps even the front bead in your peripheral vision, but if you shift focus from the target to the gun, even for an instant, you automatically slow your swing or stop the gun altogether. In shooting, your leading hand points where your eyes are looking, and our eyes can't focus on two things at the same time, especially if they're at different distances. Taking away the visual reference of a moving target gives the eyes nothing to follow, so they stop and the hand stops along with them.

This being the case, any sight that draws attention to itself is a disaster, constantly tempting you to look at it instead of the target. It's the equivalent of trying to read something highly technical or complex with loud music blaring in your ears, or trying to carry on two different conversations at once. Anything that distracts your attention from the target is inimical to good shooting and that certainly includes a bright, oversized, or otherwise obtrusive front sight.

The notion that any kind of sight can mitigate cross-dominance is patent hogwash. The only way to rectify the effect is to block vision in the eye that isn't looking right down the barrel. A patch of opaque tape or a smear of Chapstick on one lens of your shooting glasses can do the trick, and so can simply closing the offending eye, but a sight can't.

As for the gizmos that supposedly show you how much lead to put on an angling target, the less said the better. I've known some shooters who've tried them but never more than once.

If you think back to the best shots you've ever made—and I don't mean the Hail-Mary pokes that happened to scratch down a sixty-yard bird—I'll bet they were all purely instinctive moves made when you were so focused on the target that you weren't aware of the gun at all. If the gun truly fits and you've developed a consistent mount, you don't need to be aware of it. If your attention is where it ought to be, everything else becomes virtually subliminal.

I would further bet that at one time or another you've knocked a front bead right off, didn't notice it was missing till sometime later, and found yourself unable to say how long it'd been gone. If a sight was truly important, you'd notice its absence right away.

Not that I'd advise you to take off your sight and throw it away, unless of course it's one of those big neon abortions, in which case you can't get rid of it soon enough. But if you do, you'll no doubt replace it with a simple, unobtrusive bead. I've lost the sights from four or five guns, and despite the fact that I know they're all but useless, I've always replaced them.

Which, I suppose, should make me wonder about myself, but I've given up on that as an exercise in futility. Beside, there are more interesting things to wonder about—like, if a fly had no wings, would we call it a "walk"?

13

ENGLISH PROOF
OF ARMS

Over the past few years, American shooters have grown particularly interested in gun proof, and especially English proof. I can well understand this. For one thing, there are more English guns for sale in the United States at better prices than ever before. For another, the whole notion of standardized national gun proof is somewhat alien to the American scene, because we are virtually the only important arms-producing country on earth that has neither a code of proof laws nor a national proof house.

In some ways, this is a pity. The American trade wouldn't necessarily produce stronger, more reliable guns if we had a proof house; in fact, American makers do their own proof testing, and I doubt that any guns in the world are more durable than ours. But a national proof house supported by appropriate legislation certainly would relieve armsmakers from a lot of the product-liability lawsuits they're plagued with, and for that alone it's a mystery to me why the industry hasn't coalesced its efforts and resources to help establish one. Uniform proof law also would provide recourse against shady dealers who sell weak, faulty, or otherwise unsound guns.

But that's a subject for another time. Elsewhere in the world, especially in Europe, independent proof testing of firearms goes back almost to the beginning of firearms themselves. The earliest system appears to have been established at St. Étienne, the traditional gunmaking center of France, early in the sixteenth century. The English system began about a hundred years later and became official on March 14, 1637, when King Charles I granted a royal charter to the Worshipful Company of Gunmakers of the City of London, thus establishing a guild for the gunmaking trade. Among other things, the charter authorized the Company to establish standards of quality for its products and a system by which those standards could be enforced.

The charter also granted the Company complete control over all firearms made or sold within a ten-mile radius of the City of London. This meant the original square-mile, walled section of the city, not the entire megalopolis of today, but in effect it gave the Company authority over most of the armsmaking and arms-buying population. Later legislation extended its purview to include all arms made or sold anywhere in Britain.

To centralize its operation, the Company in 1713 built the London Proof House near the old City, not far from the Tower of London. The structure was rebuilt in 1757, and it's still there today, at 48 Commercial Road.

For more than 150 years, it was the only official proof house in Britain. A few Birmingham gunmakers privately set up their own, but the laws still required that all guns be proven in London. Because this included military weapons as well as sporting arms, Britain's ever-growing colonial expansion and other military activity soon created an enormous bottleneck. Though the Birmingham trade several times petitioned Parliament for authority to establish an official proof house there, the London guild, loath to give up its monopoly, managed to thwart the attempts until early in the nineteenth century. Finally, with Britain simultaneously fighting the Napoleonic Wars in Europe and the War of 1812 in America, the whole thing grew so absurd that Parliament capitulated and in 1813 established the Birmingham Proof House. In 1978, a branch proof house was authorized at Manchester.

Gun proof is one of the world's oldest forms of consumer protection. As the British rules put it, "Proof is the compulsory and statutory testing of every new shotgun or other small arm before sale to ensure, so far as is practicable, its safety in the hands of the user." Although the language appears to single out shotguns in particular, proof requirements actually apply to every sort of explosive-operated device at least in England, where "small arm" includes "shotguns, rifles, pistols, revolvers, cattle killers, line throwers, signal pistols, alarm guns, and nail-driving or other industrial tools." The requirements for proof apply to every such item sold in the U.K., not just those actually built there, so every gun, new or old, that's imported to Britain for resale must be approved and stamped by the Proof House. Moreover, when a gun is altered in any way that might affect the integrity of its barrels—reboring beyond certain limits, rechambering, or the like—it must be proofed all over again.

Both the standards of proof and the marks used to identify them naturally have changed over the years, as ammunition evolved from the use of black powder to modern nitro powders. Parliament passed Gun Barrel Proof Acts in 1868, 1950, and 1978; the Proof House itself has periodically issued updated Rules of Proof, the most important of which came in 1925 and 1954. More recently, British proof has gone metric, which set all the archtraditionalists, myself included, howling. As one English craftsman said to me, "Tons per square inch makes sense; what the bloody hell is a BAR?"

Regardless of how the various measurements are expressed, there are essentially two types of English proof, provisional and definitive, both of which involve a combination of eyeball scrutiny by the Proof Master and actual pressure-testing with ultra-heavy loads. For the most part, provisional proof applies

1

2

3

4

only to shotgun barrels in an early stage, bored but not necessarily chambered, and its purpose is to make sure the tubes are sound before the gunmaker goes ahead with the laborious and expensive process of turning them into finished barrels. The provisional marks are as follows: [1] London, [2] Birmingham. These have been in use since 1856.

Definitive proof is required of all small arms and may be performed when a gun is still in the white or completely finished. British makers typically send new barreled actions to the Proof House before they go to the stockers; imports and older guns needing reproof are usually taken off the wood before proving, since stocks aren't meant to absorb the degree of stress involved.

Definitive proof comprises a variety of marks, and even though I'm talking only about shotguns, space won't allow me to cover every one that's been used in the past 130 years, only those you're most likely to see on guns of a shootable age.

The one exception is the so-called View mark, applied to barrels and actions after careful visual inspection by the Proof Master. The London View mark [3] dates from 1672. The Birmingham Proof House used one version [4] from 1813 to 1904 and another [5] since 1904.

Some marks are almost self-explanatory, such as the words "NITRO PROOF" and "CHOKE." They mean just what they say—that barrels so marked were made for use with nitro powder and were bored with at least .004-inch constriction at the muzzle. The "CHOKE" stamp was first used about 1887. Nitro proof was instituted in 1896 as an optional level of testing and became a standard part of definitive proof in 1925. Special marks for nitro proof were devised about 1904. The original London marks [6] on the action and [7] on the barrels are still in use. Under the 1925 Rules, the Birmingham nitro-proof mark was a crown over the letters NP; in the 1954 Rules this was changed to a crown over BNP, for both action and barrels.

5

Obviously, these are important marks to look for on any gun you intend to shoot. If you don't find them or the words NITRO PROOF, or both, the gun was proven for black powder only; firing any modern, smokeless-powder cartridges in it could be a big risk.

6

Numbers such as ⅞, 1⅛, 1¼, and so on indicate the maximum shot charge the gun was intended to fire; these have been stamped on barrels since the turn of the century.

Numbers 2½", 2¾", and such indicate chamber length. This, too, is an old practice, and if a gun is rechambered and subsequently reproven in England, the new length is added among the stamps. This can get rather involved; I've seen a couple of English guns, originally built with two-inch chambers, that were

7

rechambered twice, first to 2½ inches and then to 2¾ inches, and are so stamped.

The 1954 Rules instituted the practice of stamping barrels with the maximum mean service pressure they were meant to withstand. As the current Rules define these terms, "Service Cartridge means any cartridge generally available in the United Kingdom for use by the public.... Service Load means the load...intended for use in safety in a barrel or arm. Service Pressure means the mean pressure developed by firing Service Loads." The stamp itself is a number followed by TONS PER □ ". Exactly how many tons depends upon gauge and cartridge length. Brand-new guns now show these figures as BARs, which is a formula for expressing pressure in kilograms per square centimeter.

Until 1954, barrels were stamped with gauge numbers 12, 16, 20, and so on. Under the old rules, the marking system involves a couple of things that contribute a certain degree of mystery and confusion.

One is the so-called "diamond mark" [8], which is a gauge number inside a diamond. In some cases, the number appears all alone, but in others you'll notice the letter C underneath. This often is assumed to stand for "choke"; in fact, it stands for "chamber," because the diamond mark is an indicator of chamber size. It's been around since 1887, and the date offers a clue to understanding what it all means.

In the days of muzzle-loaders, gun barrels were bored to the same inside diameter from end to end, and the exact dimension could be anything the barrelmaker wanted: 12-bore, 13-bore, 14, you name it. The shooter obtained an adequate gas-seal simply by using a patched ball or ramming a swatch of wadding in between powder and shot.

This changed with the advent of breechloaders, because breechloaders require a standardized cartridge case and a chamber in the barrel to hold it. Making cases for every bore size clearly was impractical, so gunmakers adopted even–numbered intervals as nominal gauges. Consequently, "12-gauge" actually covers two sizes—true 12-bore and 13-bore as well. So a diamond mark that contains 12 over C indicates a barrel chambered for a 12-gauge cartridge, though actual bore size might be 13-gauge.

The 1925 Rules of Proof kept the diamond mark but added another system for indicating actual bore size. If a barrel was bored within tolerances centered on .729-inch, it was simply stamped 12, but if bored larger, nominally .740-inch, it would be stamped 12 over a horizontal bar over 1. If bored on the tight side, nominally .719-inch, it would be stamped 13 over bar over 1; tighter yet, at .710-inch, it was marked 13.

The same system applied to the other nominal gauges. A 16-gauge chamber, for instance, accommodates a whole range of actual bore sizes—.669-inch (16/1), .662-inch (16), .655-inch (17/1), .649-inch (17), and .637-inch (18).

Although it was by no means a bad system, the Proof House eventually decided to simplify matters, and under the 1954 rules, guns were stamped with nominal bore sizes expressed in decimal thousandths of an inch, as in .729", .662", and .615". Now, of course, bore size is expressed metrically.

One last important point. Any gun can be submitted for reproof. One originally built for black powder can be reproven for nitro, and a modern gun must be reproven after alteration. If it passes the Proof Master's inspection, it'll be put through the proof process and, if it passes that, stamped with the reproof mark. This is a crown over the letter R—a script R for the London House and a block letter in Birmingham. About 1972, the London House began the additional practice of stamping guns with the date of proof or reproof. Typically located on the left barrel flat at the breech, these stamps comprise the letters LP, for London Proof, over a horizontal bar over a two-digit number representing the year.

The reproof mark can be valuable both in its presence and its absence. If, for instance, you're thinking of buying a 12-bore gun stamped 1⅛ or 3-tons mean service pressure but with

2¾-inch chambers, look for the reproof; if it's not there, the barrels could be unsafe.

On the other hand, finding evidence of recent reproof on a lovely old turn-of-the-century sidelock can mean that the barrels, at least, are likely to serve you well in the game fields for another ninety or hundred years. That's what they were built for, and the proof system is your assurance that they were properly made and built to last.

14

COMING
CLEAN

Gun-cleaning, like lawn-mowing, is an exercise that accommodates multiple facets of human behavior. Some don't do it at all; others do it for its own sake; and yet others do it as the means to an end.

One extreme represents a state of denial. I used to shoot skeet with a chap who hadn't run a cleaning rod down a gun barrel since the Eisenhower Administration and had no plans to do so in the foreseeable future. Every so often, he'd open his pocketknife, ream layers of wad fouling thick as orange peels out of the muzzles, and let it go at that. He was the sort who palms off yard work on children, spouses, or lawn-maintenance companies.

At the other end of the spectrum are the guys who are positively anal about it: You know, guys who check their grass daily with a spirit level, lavish their lawns with sprinklers and chemical encouragement, and burn about 200 gallons of

gasoline every summer all to find nirvana in the act of end-
lessly circling the same piece of ground like slow, noisy
buzzards.

These are guys like the three I ran into at a dove-shooting
lodge in Mexico a few years ago. Twice every day, at lunchtime
and following the afternoon shoot, they disassembled their guns
on a table in the cantina, hauled out a suitcaseful of cleaning
tools, rags, brushes, and more vials, jars, bottles and spray cans
than you'd see in a ten-stall beauty salon, and fussed over the
guns as if about to put them up for sale at Tiffany's. I've never
seen anything quite like it.

In the middle are those whose objective is simply to have a
clean gun or a mown lawn, and if accomplishing that means
performing some uninspiring or even distasteful labor, so be it.
The result is worth the trouble. You might call this the well-
adjusted approach (I do, anyway, because it's my approach, and
there's nothing peculiar about me).

Years ago, guns needed all the cleaning they could get,
especially in the days when the composition of priming chemi-
cals included some corrosive mixtures, and even later, when
powder residues were more prone to attract moisture than they
are now. That's why a lot of old guns have pitted bores, chambers, and breech faces. Now, cartridges are completely non-
corrosive, and with one exception that I'll get to in a moment,
ammunition is no longer much of a factor in how or how
often guns need to be cleaned.

To put it another way, the bore no longer needs to be the
main focus of gun-cleaning. For a game gun in normal use, it's
generally enough to swab the barrel with Hoppe's No. 9, let it
stand a few minutes, make a couple of passes with a close-
fitting bronze brush, run patches or scraps of cloth down the
bore till they come out clean, and finish up with a light coat of
oil from a patch or swab.

(And always work from the breech-end. With a non-
takedown repeater, it's tempting to go in from the muzzle, but
if you do you'll shove all the crap in the bore right into the

action. If you can't dismount the barrel, use a pull-through cleaner rather than a rod, and pull it out the muzzle.)

Sooner or later, you're going to have to deal with wad fouling, sooner for target guns, later for game guns. As I've said elsewhere in this book, the one-piece polyethylene wad is the best thing that's happened to shotgunning since the breechloader, but there's one price to pay. Heat from burning powder softens the plastic just enough that a bit of it wipes off onto the bore, especially in the forcing cones and choke cones. As this happens with every shot, fouling builds up layer by layer, and if it gets thick enough it can actually raise pressures slightly at one end of the barrel and tighten the choke at the other. Moisture that gets trapped underneath can start eating into the steel, looking for a way out.

Trouble is, the damn stuff sticks like paint and it's impervious to most of the traditional solvents. Until a few years ago, a swatch of steel wool on a rod chucked into an electric drill was about the only way to scour it out. Now there are solvents to dissolve it, though they tend to involve some fairly hairy chemistry. Gumout, an automotive solvent, works okay, as do some similar products in the "upper engine cleaner" genre. My favorite is a compound called Rayne Kleen, which is available in both organic and inorganic forms from Rayne Chemical Company, P.O. Box 151, Hermitage, Tennessee 37076, phone 615-883-2962.

Apart from wad fouling, the most serious threats to your gun's well-being these days are environmental. A gun that's been outdoors all day in even the pleasantest weather accumulates dust and chaff, possibly a bit of sand and, on a warm day, some sweaty handprints. Dust and sand are highly abrasive, and sweat is a ticket to rust.

And then, on a good or very bad day, there's blood. Whether it comes from birds, dogs or yourself, blood is as corrosive to gun steel as saltwater (it essentially is saltwater, chemically), and you can save yourself grief by taking care to wipe off any that gets onto your gun, and onto your hands and gloves as well.

At the end of even the mildest day, it's a good idea to break down your gun and wipe or brush away the dust, especially from places where metal meets metal: the barrel lumps and hook, the hinge pin, action knuckle and fore-end iron, ejectors and breech face, the breechbolt of a repeater. An old toothbrush is great for reaching the corners and crevices. Use a bit of Hoppe's to dissolve any oil or grease that might trap dust and sand, and be sure to wipe it all out with a dry cloth. Let dust and sand accumulate in oil and you've created a sludge that's as abrasive as grinding compound.

Don't stay home just because it's a rainy or snowy day, and don't panic if your gun gets wet. Water is not the dire threat you might imagine, at least not if you take the proper steps to turn a wet gun into a dry one. And the better the gun, the more impervious it is to moisture, because the better the gun, the closer the fit among all the parts. If water were the kiss of death, guns could not exist in Scotland, much of England, the Upper Midwest, the Pacific Northwest, or a lot of other places.

I keep a roll of paper toweling in my car and use it liberally at the end of a rainy day. If you're hunting in a state that doesn't require guns to be cased in vehicles, don't if it's wet. If you have to case it, blot up all the moisture you can beforehand. Either way, get it home as soon as you can, break it down, blot it thoroughly with more paper towels, and run a swatch or two of toweling down the bore.

The important thing is to let it air-dry. Don't hose it down with any so-called "moisture-displacing" junk, and don't even think about oil. If you feel you absolutely must do something, a can of compressed air, available in any good camera shop, will help drive moisture out of the nooks and crannies, or you can warm the metal with a hair dryer to promote evaporation. (Just keep that heat away from the wood, because you can bubble the finish of a lot of factory guns.) Still, air-drying at room temperature is the key and it may take several hours, so try not to be impatient. Overnight isn't too long to leave a gun that you've carefully blotted dry.

If you're out on a cold day, it's wise to let your gun stand for a while before oiling it, simply because bringing a cold gun into a warm house causes ambient moisture to condense on it.

An unfortunate number of shooters seem to think cleaning and oiling are the same thing. They aren't, and too much oil can be as bad as none at all, or in some cases, even worse. Petroleum-based oils are fine for metal, but they can literally rot gunstocks. Too much oil can gum up lockwork and ejectors as it accumulates dust, and it can stiffen so much in cold weather that things quit working altogether.

And one very important point: Hoppe's No. 9 is neither lubricant nor protectant but rather a solvent, and you should never leave a coat of it on a gun, neither in the bore nor on the outside, because it goes right on working at dissolving some-thing, like the steel itself. It's also been known to attack tradi-tional rust-bluing. Use No. 9 for cleaning, but be sure to wipe it off immediately.

A thin coat of light oil is all a working gun needs, inside or out. A drop or two of more viscous oil like Rangoon or Nevarust on the barrel lumps, hinge, and fastening bites will help smooth up the action of a newer gun as it shoots in. Grease, which some shooters like to use on hinge joints and fasteners, is actually better for protection during storage than as workaday lubrication. The thicker the lubricant, the gunkier it becomes as dust gets mixed in. English gunsmiths like to use Young's 303, but frankincense and myrrh can be easier to find here. (Years ago, I read a magazine story in which the author solemnly declared "whale sperm" to be a sovereign lubricant for guns, but I imagine that's even harder to come by. Besides, sperm-whale oil actually is a cutting oil used in lapping barrels and a quenching oil for hardening and tempering springs and other parts.)

A word about the various high-tech, super-duper lubri-cant-protectant compounds: Don't. WD-40 and the ilk are great for a lot of things, but not for guns. Many of them leave a residue that gets gummy, sticky, and difficult to remove as it accumulates. Armor-All and Son Of A Gun are blessings for automobiles, but for guns they can become a son of a bitch.

As I suggested at the start, gun-cleaning is for most of us a necessary chore and not a hobby in itself, which is also why lawn tractors are built with multi-speed transaxles. At the end of a day, getting my dog dry and fed, my boots into some warm spot, and finding a large glass of whisky and a hot shower for myself are the main priorities. To minimize the time I have to spend dinking around with my gun, I've set up a little assembly-line arrangement out in the shop—four cleaning rods, one fitted with a wool mop for solvent, one with a bronze brush, one with a slot-tip for patches, and another with a wool mop for oil. Five minutes, and the job's done.

Now this is fine for home, but taking along even one cleaning rod is a pain in the butt when you're traveling. For road trips nothing can beat The Whole Kit and Kaboodle, a yard of plastic-coated cable with brass fittings for a T-handle, bore brush, slot-tips, and such. All this along with solvent, patches, and bore adapters fits into a little round, zippered case no larger than a fly reel. A lot of sporting-goods stores carry these outfits, but if your local ones don't, contact the manufacturer, Otis Products, at 800-426-6693.

No matter where you are, the most all-around useful gun-cleaning item any shooter can have is a handkerchief-sized piece of cotton cloth soaked with about a teaspoonful of gun oil. (If you keep it in a zip-lock bag or a screw-top jar, it'll stay dust-free and won't bleed oil on anything else.) Even if you don't have the time, equipment, or inclination to do any other sort of cleaning, a wipe-down with this at the end of the day will keep your gun spiffy and free of rust. Silicone-impregnated wipers are fine, too, though nothing protects quite as well as oil.

Even if you have the proper screwdrivers and can use them without buggering screw slots, it's not a good idea to take your guns apart every time you clean them. For one thing, guns don't usually need it, and for another, the more times you take the metal parts off the wood, the looser the inletting becomes.

Unless your gun's been underwater or dunked in mud, it's best not to disassemble it more than once a year.

On the other hand, it's an excellent idea to send or take it to a gunsmith at least every two years for a professional strip-and-clean job. He'll take it to pieces, clean all the parts, polish away any corrosion that's coming on, check everything over to make sure it's working right, reassemble and lubricate it. Besides getting a thoroughly clean gun, this is a great way to ferret out any small problems before they become big ones.

If you're like me, you fool with your guns year-round, so routine cleaning and wiping are about all you need to do. But if you store your guns for a period of months, you'll want to

take some precautions to make sure they stay safe till you un-
store them. These needn't be elaborate, but you should make
sure the guns are clean inside and out, and that the innards are
lightly oiled. To protect the exterior surfaces of the metal, wipe
on a coat of heavy oil—again, Rangoon or Nevarust, which
won't evaporate as some lighter oils tend to do.

Possibly the worst thing you can do is drench the action in
oil and then stand a gun upright in a cabinet, safe, or closet so
that the excess drains down into the head of the stock and gets
a case of oil-rot started. (And even if you don't over-oil it, the
weight of the gun can in time collapse the butt pad, so there's
something to be said for storing guns butt-upwards.)

Because rust never sleeps, moisture is the major enemy
during storage, and even high humidity is enough to induce
corrosion. Storing guns in cases can be problematic, and storing one in a fleece-lined case can be a disaster. Natural fleece
and some synthetics absorb and trap moisture, and if you've
never seen a gun rusted so badly that the case has to be cut
away, take my word that you don't want to, especially not one
of your own. Felt-lined trunk cases are usually okay, though
felt also can absorb moisture. If you do store your gun in a
trunk case, toss in a couple of packs of silica gel, just to be on
the safe side, and take care to check it every month or so.

A gun safe is of course the best storage of all, both for
protection and security. But do be sure to put a jar of silica gel
or some other desiccant inside, because a safe can turn into a
sweat-box in hot, humid weather.

Now I've written all this for that middle-ground group of
shooters I described at the start. Non-cleaners probably didn't
bother to read more than a paragraph or two, so there's no
point in saying anything to them now. As for you compulsive
cleaners, please don't take anything I've said as criticism; everybody needs a hobby, and gun-cleaning is as good as any. But
if you still need something to do once your guns are pristine,
come on down to my farm—I have about two acres of grass
that almost always needs mowing.

Part II

SHOOTING

MORE CRAFT, CARTRIDGES,

AND CONTROVERSIES

CRAFT

15

FEETS, DON'T FAIL ME NOW

In the Fieldsport Shooting Schools that Bryan Bilinski and I teach together, we focus on four fundamental elements: foot position, posture, ready position, and gun mount. Almost every aspect of successful shooting derives from, or fits into, these basic concepts.

One of the elementary principles of engineering has it that structural stability depends upon a solid foundation. For anything terrestrial, you might say that whatever goes on up above is profoundly influenced by what's at ground level. Without a good foundation, no building larger than a doghouse is likely to function as it should, and any shooter not solidly balanced on his feet isn't going to be very successful at hitting his targets. You can do everything else perfectly, but if your feet aren't where they ought to be, you are, to use the plus-perfect subjunctive, scrod.

Where they ought to be is in the same plane as your hips, no more than shoulder-width apart, with the leading foot—the left one for a right-handed shooter and the right one for a lefty—slightly in advance and pointing right to where you're going to kill the target. Equally important, that leading foot should be bearing the majority of your weight.

Sounds simple, and it is, but look around at any trap, skeet, or clays club. You'll see guys with their feet so far apart that you expect to hear their Jockeys rip, braced up as if they expected the gun to knock them down when they pull the trigger. You'll see guys with their back feet directly behind the leading ones and cocked at right angles. You'll see guys in all sorts of godawful contortions, none of which is doing them any good and most of which will be the cause of at least half the targets they miss.

Spreading your feet far apart is useful if you're in a refrigerator-catching contest, and dropping your rear foot straight back and turning it ninety degrees creates a stable platform for shooting a rifle, but that kind of stability isn't worth a damn for shotgunning; it's solid but too restrictive. To catch and pass a moving target, you need to be flexible, need to move your body from the ankles, at times even pivot on your toes, and you can't do that unless your feet are fairly close together and lined up with your hips. If they aren't, you'll soon reach the limit of your ability to pivot, cramp your body, drop one shoulder or the other, and swing the gun in a rainbow arc that pulls the muzzle off the target's line of flight.

Spreading your feet or placing one behind the other also prompts you to put your weight on your back foot, and that, too, vastly diminishes your ability to pivot and swing.

The drawing on page 113 shows the right way of placing your feet. That much is self-explanatory, but how and when your feet get to where they should be is another matter.

If you're shooting targets, you can set yourself up ahead of time. You know where the target's coming from and where it's going, and if you've given the shot any thought at all, you have a good idea of where you plan to shoot it. That zone, which clay shooters call the break-point, is where you want to point your leading foot.

It works the same way when you're shooting game, but birds don't always flush at the most opportune moment, nor always go where you expect them to. Even so, you almost always have a moment or two to position your feet in the right place. You need to get squared up to the target and get yourself in balance and there's a way of doing both at the same time.

Call it The Step. It's an old English pheasant-shooter's technique that Jack Mitchell taught me, and which I've taught to quite a few others. You start with your feet together, and as the first movement in the swing-and-mount sequence, you simply step with your leading foot right toward the target. It's not a big step, no more than six or eight inches, but when your foot goes to the target, followed by your leading hand, which is followed in turn by your trigger hand, everything comes together.

You feel completely focused on the target, both mentally and physically, and by stepping in the direction you plan to shoot, you automatically put your weight on the proper foot and square your body up to where it's balanced and in a position that gives you the greatest latitude for moving the gun.

Apart from learning the technique of moving your leading hand first and keeping your head dead-still, this is probably the most effective trick a game shot can use. Though you don't really need it for clays or skeet, a clays course or skeet field is a wonderful place to practice it until it becomes second nature.

A lot of our shooting-school clients are bird hunters who shoot clays only to sharpen their skills on game, and for many of them, learning The Step has been a revelation. It works for everything—quail, pheasants, grouse, woodcock, doves, you name it—and you'll be surprised at how quickly and effectively you can get yourself into action if you make it a habit.

If you're hunting with pointing dogs and your partner goes in to flush the birds, all you have to do is stand with your feet together, ready to step toward any bird that flies your way. When it's your turn to flush, the first thing to do when the bird comes up is bring your feet together and then step toward its line of flight; it takes only a moment, but it gets your body focused where it needs to be. And taking that moment to do something positive also helps keep you from rushing and simply poking a shot at a bird that's too close. It works the same way, and confers the same benefits, when you're hunting with a flusher or walking up birds without a dog.

Bottom line is that even though you hold the gun with your hands, your feet often make the difference in how effectively you shoot it. Try using The Step as you shoot targets this summer, and see what a difference it makes.

That's not to say there won't still be times when a woodcock goes off while you're too tangled in the alder whips to do anything but howl, or times when doves drive you so off-balance that all you can do is shoot holes in the sky. But if the birds didn't win now and then, this thing we call "hunting" wouldn't be so lovely or so mysterious.

16

Assume
the Position

As I said in the previous chapter, Bryan Bilinski and I break down the act of shooting into four parts, and that's what we teach in our Fieldsport Shooting Schools: Stance, Posture, Ready Position, Swing and Mount. Bryan bases his approach firmly in Robert Churchill's method, and I suppose I do, too, although mine is so heavily influenced by Jack Mitchell and a few things I've come up with on my own that it doesn't fit any classification very neatly. If you insist on putting a name to what Bryan and I have developed between us, you could call it the Fieldsport Method.

It starts with a proper stance, which I've already outlined, based on the proposition that unless your body is in balance, your ability to swing a gun is seriously compromised.

Posture and ready position follow from there. Just as a good golf swing is built from the ground up, so is good shooting technique. If your feet are in the right place, then your body can be in the correct posture and once that's accomplished, you can build a physical relationship with the gun that allows you to make an effortless, efficient, highly effective swing and mount.

Take a lesson from any good instructor, and you'll hear the same thing over and over: Lift the gun to your cheek without moving your head, and lead with your forward hand. Keeping your head still is crucial. Any exercise in eye-hand coordination that involves accurate pointing requires something to serve as a solid point of reference. You can move your eye or your hand, but not both. Because shotgunning involves a moving target, your eye obviously has to be the stable foundation, and you accomplish that by keeping your head still. Slamming the gun butt to your shoulder and dropping your head to the stock while searching around for a target to chase is a sure ticket to a miss.

The trick to not moving your head is to have your body in the right posture to begin with. In clay shooting, you do this before you call for the target; in hunting, you do it at the same time you bring your feet to a position that provides balance and focus on the bird. Either way, it's a matter of preparing your body to receive the gun before it reaches your cheek and shoulder, not afterwards.

So what's the proper posture? Look around any target field and you'll see for damn sure what it isn't. Because trap shooters are best served by handling their guns like rifles, they tend to stand well upright, even if they often place their feet in positions that couldn't possibly accommodate any but going-away targets. Skeet shooters, on the other hand, often assume postures that are enough to make you think Darwin was wrong—crouched down and humped up like a chimpanzee about to bugger a football. Some world-class shots stand this way, and their success has naturally led to a pandemic outbreak of Skeeter's Crouch, but the fact is, their ability has nothing whatever to do with such grotesque posture. They'd break just as many targets and suffer a lot less lower-back and knee stress in the bargain if they simply stood on their hind legs and didn't try to wind human evolution back a few millennia. I don't know how you feel about it, but having three fused lumbar vertebrae, two steel rods surgically implanted in my lower back, and having inherited a long-standing family tradition of arthritis in my knees, I really don't need to go looking for ways to make anything hurt.

Call me silly, but I'd much rather stand up straight with my knees barely flexed, influence my weight toward my leading foot, and bend just slightly forward at the hips. Doing this inclines my head forward, too, and drops my chin about two inches below where it is when I stand perfectly upright. I could stand this way at a bus stop or in front of an elevator, and you wouldn't think it unusual; it doesn't look exaggerated, and it isn't, but it puts my upper body and head in position to receive the gun without moving anything but my arms.

(In order for this to work most effectively, you need to be using a gun that points right where you're looking when you lift it to your cheek without moving your head. Achieving this is called "gun fit," but that's a story for another time. Suffice to say at this point that there are sound practical reasons for having a fitted gun; it's not just something dreamed up by stockmakers, writers, or other people of dubious virtue.)

At any rate, nothing about this posture I've described needs to be extreme, and in fact shouldn't be. Spread your feet too far apart and you lose your ability to pivot from the ankles; lean too far forward and you lose your balance; drop your head too much and you lose the flexibility of your upper body.

Opposites are also true: Feet too close together diminish your stability; stand too upright and you'll never get the feeling of being one with the gun; keep your head too high and the comb of the stock will contact your jawbone instead of the shelf under your cheekbone, and the crack in the chops you'll get when you pull the trigger will quickly erode your interest in firing the next shot.

Simply put, a proper posture is one that looks neither like dress inspection nor a tryout for *Planet of the Apes*. It's balanced, relaxed, focused, and above all, comfortable.

Once your body is prepared to receive the gun, the next step is bringing the gun to a ready position. As we'll see in the next chapter, the swing and mount is a simple act in which economy of motion is paramount; to accomplish that most effectively, you must have the gun under control and hold it in such a way that eliminates the need for extraneous movement.

For the best ready position, simply hold the gun the way you normally do and tuck the butt under your right armpit. You should be holding the barrels or fore-end so that your left arm will be well extended when you shoulder the gun; you're going to point the barrels with your left hand, and you'll do it most accurately if your arm is extended.

Don't shove the stock way back under your arm, and don't clamp your upper arm against your ribs. Just having an inch or so of the butt under your pectoral muscle is enough. Both of your elbows should be angled out and down at about forty-five degrees. If you're shooting clays, you'll have a good idea of the path the target will take; find that elevation with your eyes and raise the barrels so you're looking right over the muzzles at the flight line. If you're hunting ground-flushing birds, hold the gun level to the ground or pointed just slightly up.

This ready position accomplishes several things. It brings the gun within a short distance of your cheek and shoulder, so you won't have to move it far, or rush, when you start the swing and mount. The barrels are in your peripheral vision from the start, so you can guide them where they need to go without taking your eyes off the target.

Most important, the ready position prevents you from lifting your right hand as your first move. Instead, you'll have to start by pushing forward with your leading hand, and that's exactly the sequence of motion you want.

Now, all this is easy on a target field, where the clay won't fly till you say so. There, you can spend all the time you want getting set up for a shot. Game birds, however, are less accommodating. They flush the moment you cross some invisible boundary that separates their confidence in camouflage from the panic zone, and the crossing doesn't have be physical; it can exist in sound and time as well as space. You can be ready or not, they don't care.

So what do you do, shuffle along always keeping your leading foot forward, knees flexed, head lowered, body slightly bent, and gun butt under your arm? I suppose you could, but it doesn't strike me as a good way to enjoy a tramp through the shaggy

stuff behind a dog that's scrambling like a maniac in search of that magical thread of smell. I don't walk that way when I'm hunting, and neither has anyone I've ever hunted with.

What you do is take advantage of the moment just before or just after the flush. If you walk in on a solid, pin-down point, you'll have all the time you need to get your feet, body, and gun position set. Working with a flusher, you still have a critical window in time. The best thing you can do in the first few seconds after a flush is prepare for the shot.

If you have to stop and think about where to put your feet and how to get yourself into a posture conducive to good shooting, what follows probably won't be a very effective shot, but you can train your muscle memory beyond the need for conscious thought.

Obviously you can't do it shooting game, but you can do it on a target range. Years ago, some friends and I worked out a routine for a skeet field that proved to be a superb training exercise. All it requires is having the field to yourself.

Starting on Station 1 and moving around the course, the shooter walks from the shooting pad toward Station 8, and the puller is free to release targets whenever he wants—singles, doubles, whatever, his choice. The shooter's job is to find the bird with his eyes, set his feet, assume a good shooting posture, start his gun from a ready position, and break the target, or targets. Then, he walks back from the center toward where he started and gets two more targets along the way.

You won't thank him for it at first, but the puller does you a favor by timing his pulls when you're off-step and off balance. The whole thing can be fumblesome as hell to begin with, but after a few rounds you'll start putting your stance, posture, and ready position together in milliseconds, and at that point you'll have discovered two important things. One is that when a target flies or a bird flushes, you almost always have more time than you think you do. The other is that using that time wisely in getting yourself focused and set can mean the difference between an aimless poke and a shot that makes something fall out of the sky.

17

THE SWING
OF THINGS

The past is prologue, Hamlet says. What has gone before shapes what comes after, and that should well be the case with what we've talked about here in the past couple of chapters. Proper foot placement, good posture, and having the gun under control in a ready position are all prologue to a simple, effective shooting technique, one that accommodates any target flying at any speed and angle.

So there you are, all set. Your feet are about shoulder-width apart, the leading foot pointed to the spot where you plan to kill the bird and bearing most of your weight. You're bent slightly forward at the hips, your head tipped just enough that you can simply lift the gun to your cheek by moving nothing but your arms. Your leading hand is far enough out on the gun so your arm will be well extended; the very end of the butt is tucked just far enough under your other arm that your first move has to be with the leading hand, not the trigger hand; your elbows are pointing out and down at about forty-five degrees; and you are relaxed.

What happens next should be one economical movement that combines a swing and a gun mount to deliver the end product of a shattered clay or a falling bird.

It all turns on one simple concept: Any moving object follows a specific line of flight, and if you move the gun along that line from where the target was to where it is to where it will be when the shot charge arrives, you will make an effective shot.

And it really is that simple. You can clutter things with names and methods—Churchill, Stanbury, instinctive, pass-through, pull-away, sustained-lead, everything but spot-shooting—but it all boils down to tracing lines with a gun barrel.

Imagine a target that leaves a smoke trail, or has a long tail streaming out behind. Imagine your gun as a pencil. Use it to draw a line right along the target's trail, right through the middle of the target itself, and out to a certain distance in front (we'll talk presently about how far).

Now, if accurately tracing a line is the task, it follows that whatever you do to keep the barrels on the line is good, and whatever takes your barrels off it is not.

What you don't want to do is handle your gun as you would a rifle; that is, lift it to your shoulder with your trigger hand alone. Try that sometime and watch where the muzzle goes; if you're set up properly in the first place, with the gun muzzle close to the line you expect the target to follow, raising your trigger hand makes the muzzle dip, so you're off-line from the start.

Instead, your first move should be with your leading hand, and it should start the barrel moving onto the flight line. Your first move should be the beginning of the swing. Let the actual mount follow from that.

This is very important. The swing and mount needs to be one motion, not two. Mounting the gun first and then tracking the target won't get it, even if you do move your leading hand first. Mount and swing means two moves; swing and mount is only one.

You should move this way on every target that isn't flying dead straight away from you, no matter how shallow the angle or how great—and trust me, you can shoot a gazillion targets and hunt birds for a lot of years and never see more than a handful of true straightaway shots. Almost all of them have a bit of angle involved, and if you can get into the habit of moving your leading hand toward the target from the very beginning of the shot, your shooting will improve.

There's one exception to the leading-hand-first rule. If you use The Step, as I described it a couple of chapters back (and I highly recommend you do use it for game shooting), then the step precedes the leading hand by just a bit. It's only a little step, but if you use it, the step is the first move, and your leading hand should follow it close behind.

Otherwise, I can't say it too many times or emphasize it too much: Your first move with the gun is to begin tracking the target with your leading hand. If it's a crossing target right to left, for instance, your barrel should be moving right to left before you start raising the gun to your cheek. Let your trigger hand simply follow along; its only job is to help bring the gun up. The leading hand always leads.

Think of it as pointing your finger, which we all can do very accurately. The gun barrel is simply an extension that will point wherever your finger does.

Some instructors advise practicing your gun mount in front of a mirror. I don't. It encourages a dead-gun, mount-and-swing sequence, which is one of the worst habits you can get into. Better, I believe, to pick a line—say, the junction of wall and ceiling in a room, a power line you can see through a window, whatever—and practice tracing that line with the barrel as you mount the gun. The average room is full of lines, horizontal, vertical, angling up, down, you name it; practice on all of them, moving in all directions. Work on keeping the muzzle right on each one. Through most of the sequence, you should be looking over the muzzle at the line; at the end, you should be looking right down the barrel at it. If you see the muzzle dip below the line, it means you're moving your trigger hand too aggressively. Slow it down, let it follow the leading hand.

The more you rehearse this move, the more instinctive it'll become. Ten minutes every day isn't too much. And practice the whole process every time. Set your feet, assume the right posture and ready position, and then make your move. It works best when everything is integrated.

It's important to touch the target with the barrel as you swing past it, or more properly, swing through it. Again, imagine the gun is a pencil and you're going to use it to draw a line right through the center of the target. This establishes the relationship between gun and target; without it, you'll miss above or, more often, below. And once again, gun fit is crucial. The gun needs to shoot right where you look, not way high or low.

Remember the concept of moving the gun from where the target was to where it is to where it will be. To do this, you have to approach it from behind. Where it was and where it is are vital coordinates. Connect the two, extend the same line, and that's where the target's going to be.

As to the matter of how far you need to extend the line, see the next chapter.

The final step in developing a sound technique is to concentrate on the target. Our eyes can't focus in two planes of distance at once, and in tracing a moving object, your hand follows your eye. Look at the gun and you'll stop moving it, every time. If you don't believe that, try this: Next time you're someplace where you can see traffic moving in the distance, position yourself so it's crossing in front of you at right angles, pick a car, point your finger at it, and follow it with your hand. Keep your eye on the car for a while, then focus on your finger and see what happens.

Ideally, you should be so focused on the target that you're not aware of seeing the gun. You do see it, in your peripheral vision, but the less aware of it you are, the better your chance of making a successful shot.

In a way, shooting is an act of faith, of picking a spot that's nothing but thin air and firing at it in the belief that it will be occupied a few milliseconds in the future by something you want to hit. But it's not a matter of blind faith, or at least it doesn't have to be. There's always an element of Zen at work, and sometimes even a bit of luck. Developing a good technique is to embrace the Zen, but the more you work at it and the more you practice, the luckier you'll get.

18

FORWARD ALLOWANCE

From a northern-Minnesota newspaper dated January 9, 1997: "Friday, Jan. 3, a snowmobiler came up over the bank of Daggett Lake, airborne, and was hit by a pickup truck."

This brings up the matter of lead.

The fundamental concept in hitting any moving object with any other object is that one of them has to be traveling in a certain direction at a certain speed in order to arrive at precisely the same point in space where the other will be at some point in time.

In the case of two objects moving entirely at random, governed by no intent of convergence, this is called "bizarre accident." Freakish occurrence. Pure chance.

In shotgunning, it's called "lead." Forward allowance. A matter of directing a shot swarm not to where the target is but rather to where it will be when the swarm catches up. Because lead is influenced by factors that can change from shot to shot, it is largely intuitive. It is the Zen of shooting.

Under certain circumstances, lead can be reduced to a prescription of feet and inches. Look on the clubhouse walls at any skeet club and you'll likely find a chart that shows specific leads for every target at every station on the field. To make them work, you have to use what's known as the sustained-lead technique: get your gun barrel a certain distance ahead of the target, whatever the angle demands, and keep it there, moving the gun at the same speed as the target as you pull the trigger.

Sustained lead works on targets that always follow the same flight path at the same speed, as skeet targets do. Even though the prescribed forward allowances are often specific down to a matter of inches, the fact that you're usually working with a shot spread that's two or three feet wide cuts some slack in just how precisely you have to match them. Shoot enough skeet targets that the proper leads become second nature and there's no real reason to ever miss one except from a momentary lapse of concentration. That's why big-time skeet competitions are less shooting matches than endurance contests in which everybody goes out and keeps grinding up targets till somebody has a mind-fart. Whoever suffers the fewest, wins.

The trouble with sustained lead—indeed, the trouble with the whole notion of thinking about forward allowance solely in terms of distance—is that it cannot accommodate random variations in angle, speed, and distance. When every target behaves in its own way, there's nothing upon which to base prescribed leads. Sustained lead is fine in an ordered universe, but it's not worth a damn in the face of chaos, and compared with the tightly wired formality of skeet, hunting game birds is nothing if not chaotic.

Given the old wildlife-photographers' axiom that under the most carefully controlled circumstances a wild animal will do whatever it feels like doing, you won't get very far trying to keep your barrel two feet in front of a grouse that's weaving a popple thicket or sustained-leading a woodcock that's rowing in all three dimensions at once. Eighteen inches of forward allowance might be just the ticket for a ten-yard pheasant, but not much good on one that gets up at forty. Thanks to our dogs we often have a fairly good idea of where a bird will come from and sometimes even a vague notion of where it'll go, but beyond that every flush is a new ballgame, and you'll be much better prepared to deal with that if you think of forward allowance in terms of gun speed rather than simply distance.

I can't put it any more succinctly than my old friend Jack Mitchell does when he says, "Lead is speed, and speed is lead." As Jack is, to my mind, the best shooting instructor alive, anything he says is worth thinking about, and in this case, the more you think about it, the more sense it makes.

In order to hit anything, the shooter has to accommodate the target, and by that I mean he has to take account of its flight path, speed, angle, and distance in order to accurately determine the point in space where shot swarm and target will meet. If time weren't a factor, you could do this with instruments and a calculator, mathematically find that point with gnat's-whisker precision, draw a careful bead on it, and be right on the mark.

But time is a factor. Neither a clay target nor a game bird permits much leisure; you have to kill it within a few seconds or you won't kill it at all. Fortunately, the splendid little computer inside your skull is fully capable of performing all the necessary calculations in a very short time, of directing your eyes to just the right place, and of allowing you to point your finger, or a gun barrel, exactly where your eyes are looking. If we couldn't do this, there would be no such thing as shotgunning.

Having this capacity, however, can tempt you into spot-shooting—to simply pick a spot where you think the target will be and fire at it. Sometimes you'll be right, but more often you'll be wrong, especially if your target is a live bird that has some ideas of its own about where it's going. Spot-shooting doesn't really accommodate the target, but rather attempts to second-guess it.

In order to get shot and target together, you first have to get gun and target together, and the best way to do that is to move the gun with it, to get the barrel onto its flight path, trace it, and extend that imaginary line past the target a distance sufficient to account for the time it will take your shot swarm to get there. It sounds complicated, but it really isn't; in fact, it's easier to do than it is to describe.

In this method of shooting, the gun always moves faster than the target. It has to in order to trace the path from where the target has been to where it is to where it will be. Exactly how much faster it moves depends upon who's swinging it, but in any case, gun speed is crucial.

Imagine a target crossing at right angles, moving at a steady pace. The shot swarm will travel at a given speed determined by its weight and the powder charge behind it, and will require a specific amount of time to cover the distance from shooter to target. By factoring target speed and shot speed you can calculate exactly how far ahead the gun must be if the gun is moving at the same speed as the target. This is where the sustained-lead prescriptions come from.

But now imagine that the gun is moving faster than the target. If it's moving only a little faster, wouldn't the necessary forward allowance be just slightly less than when gun and target are going at the same pace? And if the gun's moving a lot faster, wouldn't the necessary allowance be a lot less?

In fact, no. The actual allowance is the same but the perceived lead is not, and therein lies the key.

Shooting is as much art as science. Art is in many ways a matter of perception, and in any exercise involving eye-hand coordination, perception is paramount. Changing the speed of the gun doesn't change the distance or the speed of either the target or the shot swarm, so the swarm needs the same amount of time to cover the same distance. But changing the speed of the gun certainly changes what the shooter sees, and what the shooter sees is what prompts his brain to tell his finger to pull the trigger.

So let's say a sustained lead on this target requires the shooter to see the gun four feet in front when he takes the shot. Increasing gun speed by half decreases what he needs to see by just as much. The gun has to be in the same place when the shot swarm leaves the muzzle, but the faster-moving gun will get there sooner. This means the shooter has to pull the trigger sooner, using what looks like relatively less lead; otherwise, he'd miss way in front.

Which is exactly what happens on a lot of quartering shots, especially at the shallower angles, from almost straight-away to, say, about thirty degrees. The necessary forward allowances are very small, mere inches, and it's incredibly easy to overswing, allow momentum to take the barrel too far past the target, and miss it in front. On these shots, too much swing and too much gun speed are exactly what you don't need, even though they're shots that tempt us to rush, because a quartering bird or clay looks as if it's going to escape right now.

If you can resist the urge to hurry, you can connect on quartering shots by taking a short swing and pulling the trigger as soon as you catch up with the target. It'll look like you're firing right at it, with no lead at all, but even moderate gun speed is enough to carry the muzzle where it needs to go. If you just can't force yourself to slow down, you may even have to pull the trigger an instant before you catch up to the target—kill it just a second before you shoot it, as the old saying goes—but as a rule, the quicker you move on these, the less consistently you'll hit them.

Learning that there are no prescriptions for lead in clays and game shooting is sometimes a bitter pill to a beginner, especially one who's inclined to be antsy about wanting to become a competent shot overnight. Fact is, though, everybody has his own way of handling a gun, and figuring out what you need to see in order to master a variety of angles at your particular speed takes time and practice. There's no other way.

Even a veteran shot can get frustrated on those days when it seems that nothing he does is right. Often, it amounts to some problem of basic technique; not tracing flight lines properly, not raising the gun to your cheek as you should, or something similar. But it can also be a matter of moving the gun faster or slower than usual. Missing a couple of easy shots can tempt you into changing speed without realizing what you're doing; you can get spooked and start rushing, or try to be too precise and move too slowly.

Either way, your shooting will suffer, because changing speed changes everything.

19

DANCES
WITH GUNS

As I'll confess more fully in the next chapter, I have once again become a hopeless golf junkie. I knew what I was in for when I started—anguish and frustration relieved by moments of sheer ecstasy that come with the occasional well-struck shot. But I didn't know that the process of immersing myself in this utterly bizarre sport would give me new insights to the sport I have loved longest and best. I never guessed that relearning golf would lead me to better understand some aspects of shooting, but it has.

For instance: When I was a kid, Sam Snead was my hero as a golfer. I thought he had the most beautiful, most graceful, most perfect golf swing the game has ever known. I still think so. I got to watch him play an exhibition match once, about forty years ago, and remember being awestruck by the ethereal grace with which he swung the club. I've felt the same way watching Michael Jordan handle a basketball, Ozzie Smith trigger a 6-4-3 double play, and Dan Carlisle smoke clay targets flying at any distance, angle or speed. There are all kinds of ways to get any job done, but the most intriguing ones are those that transcend mere performance.

So, given my old case of hero worship for Slammin' Sam, I naturally was eager to read his new book, *The Game I Love*, and in it found a key to understanding the perfect beauty of what he did. "Everyone who knows me knows I love music," he writes. "I used my music to help me maintain my swing's rhythm. For me, waltz time, or ¾ time, was perfect for the correct golf swing tempo."

Rhythm and tempo are distinctly different qualities. One is cadence; the other, speed. But they intertwine in fundamental ways, and in their conjunction form an essential aspect of any repetitive physical skill. It's often called "timing," which I think tends to obscure an important distinction, but there's no question that it's real nor that it has a profound effect upon performance.

Rhythm in shooting is the sequence of swing and mount grooved into kinetic memory by a zillion repetitions. We develop a certain rhythm without ever knowing we're doing it. Sometimes it's a good rhythm, sometimes not. A good rhythm is a one-piece move: The leading foot goes for the target, followed by the leading hand, followed by the trigger hand, swing-mount-bang and something's broken or dead. It is a legato motion, seamless and smooth, every part connected without herks or jerks.

Poor rhythm is disjointed. Bang the gun to your shoulder, slam your cheek onto the stock, search wildly for the target, and go chasing desperately after it; swing a golf club as if it were an axe, or a tennis racket like a hammer—it's all the same. The parts don't work together, don't allow the body to move in harmony with itself nor with the tool we're using to perform a given task.

Applying to shooting what Sam Snead wrote about his golf swing, I have to agree that both acts are best performed in a three-count rhythm, waltz time: one-two-three, feet-posture-ready, move-mount-shoot.

So how do you get the feel for it? English golf instructor Martin Hall devised a lovely, if unorthodox, little exercise: Tee up eight or ten balls a few inches apart in a straight line at right angles to your stance; swing the club back and through, hitting the first; swing back without pausing, take a small step forward at the same time, and swing through to hit the second; swing back and step, hit the third; and so on. After the fourth or fifth ball, the pendulum-like motion becomes highly rhythmic and highly efficient. Every move is smooth, unhurried and, once you get the hang of it, results in meeting the ball crisply.

This struck me as something that could translate well to the gun, and it does. Try this, at home (because it looks weird) with an empty gun (for obvious reasons): From the ready position, swing, mount and click the trigger as if taking a right-to-left crossing target; swing the gun back to ready and do the same in a left-to-right motion; and repeat going the other way, all the while counting one-two-three.

"One" is the first move with your leading hand, "two" is bringing the stock to touch your cheek and shoulder at the same instant, "three" is pulling the trigger while the gun continues to swing past the target. The full sequence is one-two-three-and-one-two-three-and-one-two-three. "And" is where you return to the ready position. It'll seem awkward at first, but in a minute or two you'll find yourself swinging smoothly, purposefully, moving your hands and arms, and therefore the gun, in a simple, steady rhythm.

Keeping strictly to the three-count cadence accomplishes two things. Most important, it prevents extraneous, unnecessary movements. The most effective shooting technique is one that comprises only what's necessary for getting the job done. To attempt a moving target, you have to move the gun; to hit the target, you have to mount the gun so it points where your eyes are looking; and, of course, you have to pull the trigger. Move-mount-shoot is irreducible; you must do these things in order to shoot consistently well. But the key point here is that they're all you have to do. There's nothing you can add that will make your shooting more effective, and in fact, adding any other elements to this simple sequence is sure to make it less effective.

I have a couple of friends who have shaped their entire lives around the motto If You Don't Have To, Don't. I'm not sure how well it works in the context of a marriage or a career, but in shooting, it's the Golden Rule.

So, the three-beat rhythm accommodates what's necessary and at the same time closes the door against anything that isn't. It's also an easy way of reminding yourself what you want your body to do. If you're shooting targets, you need only run through the back-and-forth drill a few times before you set up for each shot. It's just like taking a practice swing before a golf shot, and the trick to making it work is exactly the same as in golf: Swing on the real target just as you do on the imaginary one. Golfers blow this all the time—take one or two sweet, smooth practice swings but then lunge into the ball with a grotesque lurch and end up making a terrible shot.

Too much effort is the gremlin here. Effort, Martin Hall says, ruins rhythm, and he's absolutely right. Watch a guy who's having a hard time hitting anything with a gun, and you'll see him bear down, grind his teeth, strangle the gun, lunge after the target as if he were trying to somehow fling the shot swarm himself rather than rely on the cartridge to do its work. The result is one bad shot after another, and the harder he tries, the worse it gets.

The cure is wonderfully simple. Take a deep breath through your mouth, expanding your chest as far as you can, hold it for a count of three, and exhale through your nose. Do this three times; your mind will clear and you'll relax. Then do my back-and-forth swing exercise eight or ten times and shoot the next target keeping exactly the same rhythm.

Concentrate on the rhythm and what you see, nothing else. Don't try to think your way through a shot while you're making it. As Sam Snead puts it, "You should try to hit the ball with a blank mind if possible." As one who does just about everything with a blank mind, I certainly agree. Hum or whistle a little waltz-time ditty while you shoot; it'll help keep your mind switched sufficiently off to let your muscle memory do what your hours of practice have trained it to do.

As I said at the start, rhythm and tempo are two different things. Rhythm is the cadence, the pulse of a complex, sequential physical act. Tempo is how fast you perform it, and tempo is one thing in my students' repertoire that I try not to mess with very much. If I ask an experienced shot to change anything about his tempo, it's almost always to slow it down. I might encourage a beginner to be more aggressive, which sometimes means increasing speed, but only to the point where he can find an optimum tempo in which to exercise his most effective rhythm. Even so, that tempo is never very fast.

Rushing is a form of effort, and effort ruins rhythm. Unless you've trained the hundred-gazillion hours of a Tour golfer or a world-class competitive shot, you won't be able to significantly increase your tempo and still keep your rhythm intact. If you don't believe me, go get a length of scrap lumber, a hammer and a handful of nails, and drive about ten of them at whatever tempo is most comfortable. Then try to drive a few twice as fast and see if you can pound them in as smoothly and accurately as you did before. If you can, drinks are on me next time we meet.

Instructors who immediately start tinkering with someone's tempo, trying to get him to speed up, make me cringe. Every shooter has his own best speed in handling a gun, and though it often varies according to the target's distance and angle, it is remarkably consistent overall. Unless it's so effortful as to disrupt his rhythm, or so lackadaisical that he appears to be missing targets in his sleep, it ain't broke and therefore does not need repair.

Of the two, rhythm seems to me far more important. Take away the extremes, and just about any tempo is fine, so long as it works. But a faulty rhythm will not function consistently at any speed, and when rhythm is inconsistent, so are the results. One of the best things you can do for your field shooting is spend time on a target field working on your rhythm. The back-and-forth drill trains the body. To get your mind in the right semi-blank frame, let a waltz play through your head before you call for the target, and keep it going as you swing, mount, and shoot.

And it's your choice of waltz, of course. George Strait, Johann Strauss, Willie Nelson—doesn't matter. Hear what pleases you, but hear something. You can't dance without music, and I think you'll be pleased with what happens to your shooting when you approach it in terms of dancing with your gun.

20

PERFECT
PRACTICE

After thirty years' clean living, golf has its hooks in me again. It's my wife's fault, and Gene Hill predicted it would happen.

Talking on the phone a few months before he died, I asked Gene what he'd been doing lately. Hitting golf balls, he said, for which I gave him a proper ration of grief, pointing out that golf is to one's equanimity the equivalent of herding cats. A few days later, I got a letter from him. "About golf," he said, "you're next. No true Scotsman can pass up an opportunity for self-inflicted humiliation."

Now, I'm almost certain I never told Gene that from the age of twelve till about twenty-two I ate, drank, breathed, slept, and dreamed golf, played at least eighteen holes—usually twenty-seven and often enough thirty-six—every spring, summer, and early-fall day I wasn't in school. I got fairly good at it, but after graduating from college and enrolling in graduate school, the game and I came to a parting born of too little time, too little money, and a sense of having reached the point where I should put away childish things. Gene didn't know any of that, but he proved an able prophet. Vicky decided she wanted to learn golf, and being a gallant sort, I said I'd join her in a few rounds, just to see how she liked it.

She liked it a lot. For me, it was like a former heroin addict taking one more fix just for fun.

So now I'm playing again, hitting a few hundred practice balls every week, trying, with the help of a good teaching pro named David Cheatham, to put a once reasonably graceful swing back together. It's been an object lesson in reminding me how important instruction and practice are to developing a physical skill, but even more, in driving home the point that there's practice and then there's practice.

Practice, they say, makes perfect, and that's true but only if it's perfect practice. Practice makes permanent. Imperfect practice produces imperfect results. Which is one of the sermons I preach to my shooting students.

To carry the comparison just a bit further, I'm continually impressed at how effective my golf practice is when I do it properly, and how useless it is when I don't. I try to give every shot perfect practice beginning with the preliminary ritual of standing behind the ball, picking a target and drawing a flight line, settling my grip, and setting up to the ball in a good stance and posture. Then I fix my eyes on the backside of the ball; trigger my backswing with a slight forward movement of my hands and try for a smooth take-away; hesitate slightly at the top; trigger the downswing with my hips; accelerate the club head while transferring weight from right to left; pronate my wrists through impact in search of that elegant, elusive touch of draw that shapes the ball's flight slightly leftwards; and follow through till the club shaft lies across my shoulder blades.

If I do all that every time, every shot, I can advance my ability more with one bucket of balls than I could with a thousand flailed haphazardly off the practice tee without regard to form.

Shooting is no different except that shooting is a hell of a lot simpler act than a golf swing, and easier to perform consistently well. Even so, perfect practice is the only road that approaches perfect results.

In the past few chapters, I've outlined a thoroughly proven technique for effective wingshooting. I guarantee it'll work if you learn it well, and I guarantee you'll learn it well if

you practice it faithfully. But if you don't practice it perfectly, all bets are off, all guarantees null and void except this one: indulging in sloppy, inconsistent practice virtually guarantees becoming a sloppy, inconsistent shot.

Now, by perfect practice I don't mean hitting every target you shoot at. That's the goal you're working toward, even though it won't happen no matter how much you practice. Perfect practice is the means to that end, not the end itself. I think I have my golf-practice routine refined to a reasonably high level, but I can still hit a chili-dipper now and then, chunk a fat iron, top one with the driver, bloop a lob wedge half as far as I can spit, or scuff a three-foot putt. Perfect practice doesn't mean performing perfectly; it just means practicing perfectly.

For a golfer, perfect practice means swinging a club but not necessarily hitting a ball; for a shooter, it means swinging the gun but not necessarily firing a shot. It means placing your feet and body, bringing the gun to a ready position, picking out a flight line, and tracing it with the barrels from the moment you start the swing to a moment after you've pulled the trigger. This is the sort of practice you can do at home, indoors, perhaps using snap caps to keep your feel for the trigger honed to a good edge.

It's the sort of practice you can think your way through step by step, over and over, till the whole sequence is so deeply committed to kinetic memory that you no longer have to think about what you're doing.

The key to consistent golf is a repeating swing. Watch the Tour pros on the tube, and you'll notice that every full swing they take is identical. If there's a little quirk in it, it's there every time.

Same with shooting. Watch a good shot at work, and you'll see the same moves time after time, and not just when the target's in the air. A good shot goes through precisely the same set-up ritual every time, but he's not thinking about every move he makes. He's done it so often that he doesn't have to. He's reached a point where he can concentrate his mind on one single focus. Pro golfers call this the "swing thought." I don't know if the concept has any universal term among shooters, but "shot thought" would be as good as any.

For me, vision is the key. I try to think through my eyes, concentrate on the target, let my mind otherwise go blank (which is extremely easy for me), and let my hands and arms and body handle the gun without conscious direction, depending entirely upon the muscle memory I've grooved in through years and years of repetition. When it works, it works very well, and when it doesn't—when I shoot like a man who is completely unconscious rather than just unconscious of familiar moves—the problem is either lack of visual focus or of second-guessing, of actively thinking about how I'm swinging the gun rather than trusting my body to do what it can do perfectly well so long as I stay out of the way and just let it happen.

In the Fieldsport schools, Bryan and I put a lot of emphasis on the fundamentals, drilling the basic elements to the point where we probably sound like a broken record in stereo. But we've been at it long enough to know that's the key to consistency, regardless of a shooter's level of skill or experience. The technique we teach, the same one I've outlined here, will accommodate any target at any angle, but only if you perform the entire sequence every time.

So, perfect practice means going through all the steps every time—the right foot position, the right posture, the right ready position, the right swing and mount. Like the component parts of a good gun, there are no extraneous pieces; leave out any one of them, and the whole will not function as it should. If you practice only one aspect, or two, you might get fairly good at that part, but it'll never serve you as well as it could.

I see this on the practice tee at the golf course all the time—guys hitting one ball after another as fast as they can, never appearing to change what they're doing, and likely as not making the same mistakes over and over again. If they're not actively building bad habits, they certainly aren't doing much to build good ones.

I see shooters doing the same thing, blithely ignoring the fundamentals and apparently hoping that if they just keep on keeping on, divine intervention will eventually get them where they want to be. Some seem to think that a few words of Anglo-Saxon origin hurled loudly after a missed target will cause the next one to break. (A lot of golfers favor this technique as well.)

Ironically, even perfect practice can be heir to a wee virus now and then, but that's the nature of any repetitive physical act more complicated than nose-picking. Still, the fundamental things apply. When a veteran shot comes to us with a problem, nine times out of ten it lies somewhere in the basics, some little counterproductive quirk that has crept unnoticed into the footwork, the posture, or the simple sequence of swing and mount. Fortunately, such things are usually easy to spot if you know what to look for, although the treatment sometimes calls for a bit of creativity.

My favorite case of this came in the form of a chap who went through our school a couple of years ago, a highly experienced shot who could do anything with a gun except consistently move his leading hand first. Consequently, there were certain targets he just couldn't hit except by accident. When there was plenty of time to reestablish his track on the target after getting off-line by too much trigger-hand motion, he was fine. But he couldn't catch up with targets whose flight line had to be picked up quickly and accurately right from the start, and on those he was scoring more behinds than a toilet seat.

Increasing his gun speed wasn't the answer, because speed wasn't the problem and besides, I've found that trying to change an experienced shot's tempo usually does more harm than good. The problem was an overactive right hand, and that can be one of the hardest bad habits to break. He could rein it in perfectly well in dry-practice, but the instant a target appeared, all those years of conditioning just took over. It was frustrating for him, and I was getting a bit frazzled myself, trying to come up with a solution that would stick.

I don't remember what made me think of it, but it finally occurred to me that I was dealing with a thoroughgoing leftbrainer, to whom sequence is everything. So next time his turn came up, I told him to forget about his hands and step toward the kill-point with his left foot before he did anything else and to just let his left hand follow that foot.

And glory be, it worked. His deeply logical mind keyed everything to a first move, and so long as the first move was with his hands, his old habits were unbreakable. He simply could not make the first move with his left hand, but making the *second* move with that hand...no problem. After about ten minutes of getting accustomed to the step, most of those formerly impossible targets started disappearing in puffs of smoke. He was ecstatic. I've never had any regrets over stumbling onto a way to look like a hero.

The point is that for him, perfect practice will always include that little step. I'm sure he still does the stance-posture-swing-and-mount drill we outlined for him at the end of the school. He's the sort of guy who will practice. But if he ever gets too casual about it and allows perfect practice to degenerate into mere practice, he'll be right back where he started. That applies to everyone.

But that's how golf-swing doctors and shooting instructors stay in business. Nothing's more important than perfect practice except perhaps getting a bit of help now and then to keep it perfect.

If you're a scratch golfer and a good teacher at any aspect of the game, and would like to become a scratch shot, I think we could do some barter. You'll have to talk to Bryan, because he's the business head of our schools, and he's more flinty-eyed than I when it comes to barter. That's why he's the perfect partner.

It's also why Gene used to say, "Bryan, nobody named Bilinski is Scottish. That's why there's hope for you."

21

OFF TO A
GOOD START

"My wife and I are both in our twenties," the young man wrote, "both teachers, and married just a couple of years. My other great loves are bird hunting and shooting. My wife is interested in learning to shoot. I would prefer that she learn from a professional, but there are no shooting schools in our area, and we can't afford the expense of traveling to attend one.

"My only alternative at this point is to teach her myself, but I hesitate to try. I want her to learn properly and, most of all, enjoy the experience so it can be something we share in the future. That's really important to me, because she's also my best friend."

It's been a while since I received a letter from a reader that touched me quite like that one. I know the feeling behind it, for one thing, and for another it expresses a level of sheer good sense that is truly impressive.

I do not generally recommend that husbands try to teach their wives to shoot, nor fathers their sons or daughters. Not that I'm opposed to women and young people taking up shooting; on the contrary, I believe they're vital to the future of our sport. But like the young chap who wrote to me, I want every newcomer's experience to be positive and enjoyable, and that often is not the case when the student–teacher relationship is burdened with emotional attachments and expectations and fear of disappointment and all the other baggage that can subvert the best of intentions. Good teaching and good learning are usually best accomplished when neither party has any particular emotional stake in the outcome.

But sometimes it's the only option, and as I replied to that letter with what I hope is some useful guidance and advice, it occurred to me that others—maybe you, maybe someone you know—might be facing the same dilemma. If so, maybe this will help.

Now it may seem too basic to deserve mentioning, but a good learning experience requires both a willing teacher and a willing student. And it does not go without saying that this always exists. If your wife or son or daughter or girlfriend doesn't really want to learn to shoot, you won't do anyone any good by forcing the issue. But if the interest is genuine, then the bug's on you to make it a positive experience, to nurture that interest, to keep it alive and fresh. You will, in short, have to be prepared to put forth a consistent effort. If you aren't, don't even start, because it'll come to a bad end.

If you are, remember this: In some important ways, what you teach is less important than how you go about it. The approach you take and the amount of patience you can bring to bear will profoundly influence the results, for good or ill.

Your first task is to take a good long step backward, away from some emotions that are highly destructive to good teaching. Naturally you want your spouse or your child to learn quickly and be successful, but the fact is, everyone progresses at his own pace, especially in developing a complex physical skill.

Learning to shoot takes time and practice. Don't expect your student to become a whiz-bang shot overnight; nobody does.

Above all, don't burden your student with your expectations. No matter what happens, don't make him feel that he's letting you down or that his performance is any reflection on you. It's the kiss of death to any teaching situation.

That the personal relationship between teacher and student can intrude in negative ways is the down side of the deal. The up side is that when you live with your student, you have more time and more teaching opportunities than a professional instructor who works on an hourly basis, and if you can capitalize on this in good, creative ways, the whole experience can be great fun and enormously satisfying for everyone.

Maybe it's just the way my mind works, or possibly the fact that I've spent most of my life teaching one thing or another, but I find it helpful to approach objectives in terms of their component parts. In shooting, there are three: the theory of intercepting a moving object; an efficient way of handling a gun; and effective means of putting the two together.

The theory is the simplest part of all, but don't assume that someone who's never shot before automatically understands the concept of forward allowance. One of the most useful teaching experiences I ever had came years ago in the midst of a lesson with a beginner who persisted in shooting behind everything. At some point I told her to look at the air just a bit farther ahead of the target. She turned to me with a combination of amazement and sudden understanding on her face, and said, "You mean I should be shooting *in front* of it?"

Well, yes. I felt like a dunce for assuming she knew that in the first place. Fortunately, in the excitement of suddenly being able to powder clay targets, she never realized what a stupid mistake I made; she got very happy in nothing flat, and I learned a lesson I'll never forget.

So, take the time to explain that in order to make contact with a moving object that's any distance away you have to anticipate where it's going to be when the shot gets there. If you're teaching a child, you can put some fun in it by having him roll a ball at some object you drag across the floor a few feet away.

Or set up an exercise that's good practice for any shooter at any level of skill: Hang a tennis ball on a string from the ceiling, set it swinging, and practice touching it by tracing its path and reaching out to arm's length with your forefinger extended. I know some world-class target and pigeon shots who do this as training; it's an excellent exercise of eye-hand coordination. Have him use the hand that guides the barrel. Anything you can do to help condition the kinetic memory in that hand will pay off when it's actually holding a gun.

There are two other important theoretical points to make. One has to do with speed and the other distance, and the two notions are virtually inseparable. Increasing the speed or the distance of the target means you have to move to it faster or go farther ahead in order to intercept it. You can illustrate this with either the rolling ball or the swinging ball. In the one case, back up or drag the target object faster; in the other, either swing the tennis ball harder or give your student a yardstick and have him work on touching the ball with that, still tracing its path but reaching out like a fencer.

Better yet, try it both ways. The solutions are interchangeable.

In any case, don't talk about lead as if it's a prescription. It's not. I can only shake my head when I overhear someone on a skeet field pontificating about lead in terms of feet and inches. For one thing, it works only with the sustained-lead method of shooting, and sustained lead works consistently only at skeet; for another, the average person, shooter or not, doesn't have a clue what constitutes three and a half feet at twenty-two yards when he's looking over a gun barrel. So if you want to give your student something really useful, just tell him that lead is speed. How much he needs depends on how fast he's moving the gun. The two exercises I described earlier can demonstrate that nicely.

He might find, and you might too, that it's most effective to increase gun speed in some situations and forward allowance in others. I didn't realize this until someone mentioned it during a driven-partridge shoot in Spain last winter, but I tend to vary my speed when the targets are fairly close in but keep the gun moving relatively slowly and increase my lead when they're farther out. After watching me shoot a couple of drives when the birds were flying anywhere from twenty-five to fifty yards overhead, he asked if I was purposely being more deliberate on the high ones. I wasn't, actually, but I paid more attention to what I was doing on the next few drives and discovered that while I almost always accommodate the speed of closer birds, I hit the long ones better when I increase the forward allowance I see rather than gun speed.

For me, it's just one of the grooves that time has worn, but it's something I'll suggest to my shooting students in the future. Yours might find it helpful, too.

By spending some time on these exercises and demonstrating the theory of shotgun shooting, you can accomplish quite a lot without ever having your student hold a gun, much less fire a shot.

Just as a photographer needs a camera, a shooter needs a gun. And for a beginning shooter, having the right gun is especially important because the wrong one will not only be an obstacle in the learning process but a serious damper on enthusiasm as well. As I said earlier, the most important part of teaching someone to shoot is in making it a positive, enjoyable experience, and no beginner enjoys using a gun that's too big, too heavy, too clumsy, too prone to recoil, or ballistically too demanding of skill he doesn't yet have.

It's also important that a beginner who is serious about learning to shoot should do so with a gun that's his or her own. It's okay to fool around with borrowed guns for a bit if you're not sure about your student's level of interest, but if the enthusiasm is genuine, then don't begin teaching in earnest until he has the right gun and it belongs to him.

There are several reasons for this. Having your own gun makes shooting more personal. Simple pride of ownership helps build enthusiasm and a sense of responsibility. And in the case of a young person, contributing something toward the purchase enhances the commitment.

So somebody's going to have to invest some hard cash, and as it's probably going to be you, here's something else to think about. You don't have to order a best-quality gun custom-built for your twelve-year-old, but for heaven's sake don't saddle him with some beat-up clunker that isn't worth using as a tomato stake.

About a hundred years ago, when I was a fledgling college instructor, I supplemented my meager income by giving guitar lessons at a local music store, mostly to youngsters. More often than not, they'd show up for the first session dragging an instrument that had the action of a bass fiddle and produced a quality of sound that was about what you'd get by putting strings on a bolt of firewood. When I questioned the parents about this, the response was always the same: "Oh, we'll wait a few months and see if he likes playing and then see about getting another guitar."

To which I'd suggest that giving an instrument difficult even for me to play to a beginner with small, soft fingers and undeveloped forearm muscles was pretty good insurance that their child's interest wouldn't last a few weeks, much less a few months. My best advice was to buy the best guitar they could reasonably afford, and for two reasons. One, it'll help success come easier, and two, if he ultimately decides to give it up or wants to upgrade his instrument, you'll get more of your money back selling or trading a good guitar than one that was essentially worthless to begin with.

If the first point didn't sink in, the second usually did, and it applies just as well to guns.

From a teacher's view, the first point is the most important: In learning to use an instrument—a guitar, a gun, or whatever—the instrument itself influences the level of enjoyment and the likelihood of success. It's as simple, and as complicated, as that.

Now exactly what constitutes the "right" gun depends upon the person who's going to use it. The type of gun isn't terribly important nor, with some exception, is the gauge. The key factors are size, weight, balance, recoil, and ballistics, and each one is to some extent influenced by the others.

It's probably safe to assume that your beginner is a young person or a woman, therefore relatively small physically and perhaps not possessing a great deal of upper-body strength. This means a gun that's too heavy—say more than about 6 or 6¼ pounds—will be tiring to lift and swing more than a few times running. When fatigue sets into arm and shoulder muscles, smooth gun-handling goes right down the drain.

And if it's too heavy or too long in the stock, or both, a beginner will instinctively attempt to offset the weight or length by leaning backward from the waist. That puts him way off-balance and promotes aiming instead of pointing, both of which are poisonous to good shooting.

You don't need a formal gun-fitting at this point, because a meticulous fit is of real value only when a shooter has developed a consistent gun-mount, but it's extremely important that the stock not be too long.

If your student is a grown woman, you can have her stock cut down to the right length and think no more about it. If you're working with someone who's still growing, you'll have to consider the future as well as the present. Just don't ignore stock length in the beginning and expect all to be well when he grows into the gun. He will, of course, grow into it, but by then he'll have developed so many bad habits that he'd be better off if he hadn't started at all.

You can accommodate a growing shooter in several ways. Buy an inexpensive replacement stock from one of the high-volume wood companies, have it cut to proper length, extend it with a pad as your shooter grows, and put the original stock back on when he's of a size to use it. Or have the original stock shortened, keep the sawn-off portion, and have a stockmaker put it back on slice by slice as needed.

In any event, don't think in terms of ruining a good gun if you have it cut to fit a beginner; think in terms of ruining a potentially good shooter if you don't.

You should also bear in mind that shortening the stock will change the gun's balance, and if it gets too nose-heavy, your shooter will want to lean backward, just as if it were too long. Best to get a relatively short-barreled gun to begin with, so that bobbing the stock won't disrupt the balance very much.

Recoil is, if you'll pardon the expression, a sensitive issue for a beginner. Because it's a new sensation, your shooter will be hyper-aware of even relatively mild kick at first. This will fade as he becomes accustomed to it and as he begins to concentrate on targets instead of the gun, but you'll do him a treat by not subjecting him to any more kick than necessary.

This doesn't necessarily mean you have to start with a small-gauge gun. Most women and teenagers can do just fine with a lightweight 12-bore gun if you give them very light loads to shoot in it. Both Estate Cartridge and Fiocchi make excellent ⅞-ounce 12-gauge cartridges. If a light 12 is too heavy, find a light 20 and get some ¾-ounce Estate Mighty-Lites.

Or buy a 20-bore gas-operated autoloader. Some makers—Remington, for instance—build them in Youth models with short barrel and short stock; they're excellent for beginners. You may have to use slightly heavier loads, because ¾-ounce shells may not create enough pressure to cycle some autoloading actions, but the guns' capacity for damping recoil is such that hardly anyone should find ⅞-ounce skeet loads uncomfortable.

The 28-gauge is a splendid choice for a beginner. Its ballistics are superb, on a par with the 20; recoil is virtually nil; and as most of the less-expensive ones are built on 20-gauge frames and receivers, the weight is enough to further reduce kick while the gun itself remains relatively light.

Don't even think about starting someone with a .410. It's

as bad as giving him a nine-pound Magnum 10-gauge, but for different reasons. All the .410 has going for it is a lack of kick. What's more important for a novice is that it has no pattern, either, or at least not much to speak of. If the weight and recoil of a .410 are all your beginner can handle, then you'd be far better off waiting until he's older and grown large enough to handle a gun he can actually hit something with on a consistent basis.

Now I know I have a bad attitude toward the .410, but it's because the .410 is a lousy cartridge, worthless for anything except targets and inappropriate for anyone but a good, highly experienced shot. Even that shooter will find its piddly, strung-out shot swarm very difficult to use effectively time after time.

When you're working with a beginner, effective and consistent shooting is the goal. The more targets he hits, the more fun he has; the more fun he has, the more he enjoys shooting; the more he enjoys shooting, the easier your job as teacher and the more satisfying the result.

Which brings us to the final step. The most important objective in teaching a beginner to shoot is to get your student started with a simple, effective technique that doesn't involve anything he'll need to unlearn later. Beyond that, you want him, or her, to hit as many targets as possible, and you also want to instill the concept of swinging the gun right from the start.

You can begin all this at home, indoors or out, with an unloaded gun. Describe the fact that any object moving through the air, whether it's a bird or a clay target, travels along a specific path, a flight line. Imagine it's leaving a smoke trail or has a great long tail streaming out behind, whatever helps in visualizing the flight line. The trick in shooting is simply to move the gun barrel along that line, from where the target has been to where it is, to where it's going to be a moment or two after you pull the trigger. Go back to the exercises I described in the first part of this chapter.

Don't talk about lead as a prescription; just keep emphasizing that he'll have to move the gun faster than the target's flying.

Do emphasize that his job is to point to the place where the target's going to be. Point, not aim. Point the gun barrel as if he's pointing a finger.

Don't let him slam the gun to his shoulder and then look around for something to point at. It's forward hand first, always. The other hand just follows along, lifting the gun to his cheek while his head is dead-still.

Insist that every time he mounts the gun, he must also be swinging it. Have him practice tracing lines—cabinet tops, roof lines, the junctures of walls and ceilings, whatever—always moving the gun barrel from point to point in one smooth motion, keeping the muzzle on line from the moment he starts it moving until a moment after he fires an imaginary shot.

It's impossible to overrate the value of this kind of drill. It's practice at reading and tracing lines. It's the foundation of a consistent way of swinging and mounting the gun. It's the development of certain muscles and of a level of muscle memory that are the basis of effective shooting. It is, in fact, the essence of shooting a shotgun.

Learning to swing and mount as one motion is the crucial first step, and your student should be well-schooled and well-practiced at it before he ever fires a shot at a moving target.

When you do make the transition from handling the gun to actually firing it, be very selective about the targets you use in the beginning. Do not go to a trap range or set up a portable trap and start your shooter on going-away targets. Straight-aways are dead-gun shots; there's no swing, no sense of tracing lines, just poke and shoot, and that's the last thing you want a beginner doing.

Of all the places for starting a beginner, I like a skeet field best, and there are only two presentations to use at first—low house Station 1 and high-house 7, floaty incomers easy enough to hit that I can have the rankest beginner smashing targets in about five minutes and be teaching something useful at the same time.

Besides being a dead-gun situation, a going-away target is a panic button. To a novice, it appears to be escaping so quickly that he's going to rush, lose his technique, poke at it, aim, do everything wrong and learn only frustration. An incomer, on the other hand, gets easier as it develops; it's coming toward you, getting bigger, moving slower, until finally it seems as if you can just poke your finger right through the middle of it, which is precisely what your shooter is going to do, except what pierces the target will be a charge of shot that's traveling right where his finger has pointed.

An incoming target demands a moving gun—not much, but just enough to let your student know that a moving gun is a deadly one. It requires no big forward allowance and therefore does not tempt him to measure a lead. Just have him focus on the front edge of the target as it's coming on, bring the barrel up from behind and pull the trigger the moment he sees the muzzle and the forward edge come together.

A teaching tip: No matter what the shot or how consistently your shooter is smashing them, don't give in to the temptation of watching the targets. Watch your shooter. Pay attention to his technique and be ready to point out lapses as they occur. You'll know if he hits 'em or not. The quickest way to feel like a fool when you're teaching is to have your student ask, "What did I do wrong?" and having to say, "Well, gee, I don't know; I wasn't watching you."

And don't let him get away with sloppy technique just because he happens to hit a target, and don't worry about a miss that could as easily have been a hit but for another inch of barrel movement. As my mentor Jack Mitchell has said to me a hundred times, "You missed it, but it wasn't a bad shot; don't fret."

Nothing succeeds like success. I've had beginning shooters literally dance in exhilaration at learning how easy it is, and how much fun, to smoke incoming targets. One, after reducing five straight to dust, even dropped the gun and gave me a hug—which was a mixed blessing, because the gun was mine. Fortunately she dropped it in the grass and not on the concrete shooting pad. (It's also a good object lesson in why you never allow a beginner to load more than one cartridge at a time.)

Point is, if you get someone started successfully, you've got one thoroughly hooked customer, and that makes the harder shots easier to learn. Enthusiasm, confidence, and determination can overcome almost anything.

Don't be in any rush to leave the incomers and don't hesitate to go back to them. In fact, it's a good idea to end every shooting session with a dozen easy incoming targets, just for reinforcement and a confidence boost.

After about a hundred, though, evenly divided between Low 1 and High 7 if you're teaching on a skeet field, it's time to add some angle. But not much. Just move over to stations 2 and 6 and shoot the going-away targets. They still demand a moving gun, but coach your student to swing to the target and shoot right at it without stopping the barrel. For those shallow angles, the momentum of the swing builds in lead enough.

Incomers from 2 and 6 are great. Your shooter will have to use a bit more speed or more daylight in front than he did to hit incomers from 1 and 7, but by now he should be getting the hang of it and be able to adjust. If not, go back to where you started.

Another teaching tip: Once you know your student has the technique in hand, you need only watch the gun muzzle to know what caused a miss. When they miss one behind, and ask what they did wrong, and you tell them they looked at the gun instead of the target, they think you're a wizard. How do you know? they sometimes ask. Because the barrel stopped moving. And the reason any gun stops moving is that the shooter looks away from the target and at the gun. That's just how it works.

Don't let a beginner push too far in any one session. Fifty shots at a go is usually enough. Beyond that, physical and mental fatigue will start to work against him. And try to end it on a high note, a target broken with a shot that feels as good to the shooter as it looks to you.

Stay with the easy shots until you're satisfied that your shooter has his technique under control. It may take 300 shells or a thousand, doesn't matter. Don't leave the easy ones till he's brimming with confidence. And then gradually increase the angles until you're working with ninety-degree crossers.

They'll be frustrating at first. When I started shooting skeet, right after the Civil War, Station 4 was the bugaboo of all bugaboos, and I thought the old-timers were being especially cruel to tell me it was the easiest station on the field. But then I began to notice it was the one station where they seldom missed, and not long after it became the one I seldom missed. When your beginner has trouble with it, just tell him to swing a little faster or look a little farther ahead of the target, try to miss it in front. Either way, it works.

Once in a registered shoot, I found myself squadded with a family group, father and his son and daughter, both teenagers. Dad shortly disendeared himself to me by obviously favoring his son, who was a good shot, while behaving like a jerk toward his daughter, who was a potentially great shot, saying, "Well, it's a man's game!" every time she missed.

Station 4 was her bugaboo, too. After missing both shots there in the first round, she just looked stricken. When we came off Station 3 in the second round, I held her back from the others and said, "Now listen: Swing fast on these targets and pull the trigger as soon as you see daylight in front of them."

I'll never forget the look of gratitude on that pretty young face. Nor the fact that she smoked every Station 4 target in the rest of the match, came within a few points of tying her brother, and was ecstatic. And I have to confess that I took a fiendish pleasure in shooting old Dad right out of the standings.

You have to take such care with the beginners. But it's worth every effort; they're the ones who're going to carry it on. They're our future. They're us, at some point so many years from now that we won't be here. Except through them. So let's teach them well.

CARTRIDGES

22

THE ODD SHOT
HERE AND THERE

I can remember that pheasant as if it was yesterday, a big, gaudy cockbird hammering up out of the stubble, crossing in front of me, cackling his angry invective. At twenty-odd yards on a sunny day, I could almost count his dark-tipped flank feathers. He was meat in the pot even as I started to swing. The gun boomed and socked my shoulder, and feathers flew.

So did the bird. He rocked, faltered, righted himself and pounded on. By the time I got my chin off my chest and reached for the back trigger he was well out but well in range, and I hit him the second time, too, drawing more feathers. And still he flew, down the long open slope, across a plowed field, and put down at the edge of the brush along the creek. He was just a speck in the distance, but his landing looked clumsy, and it gave me a little jolt of hope. By the time we got there he was nowhere to be seen. The Labradors rooted and rummaged with all their hearts and all to no good.

He's not the only bird I've shot and failed to recover in the fifteen years since that happened, but he's the one I always remember and the one I think about when I have occasion to muse on how little difference there can be between good shots and bad ones.

Clearly, I caught him with just the edge of the pattern— probably the bottom edge, because the gun I was using was a fair bit higher in the stock than really suits me. The feathers don't mean much; even a single pellet grazing a bird's skin can knock loose an ungodly number of them. But the fact that he almost fell tells me he was hit hard. You don't stagger a wild cock pheasant with just a love pat.

The killing power of any firearms projectile, bullet or shot, depends upon the amount of kinetic energy it transfers to whatever it hits, and energy derives from a combination of mass and velocity. Because there are practical limits to how much velocity a projectile can attain, mass is the more important factor. That's why rifle guys follow the rule of thumb that says the larger the game, the heavier the bullet needs to be. You simply can't make a very light bullet move fast enough to generate the required amount of energy.

This is also true of shot pellets, but there's even greater limitation to what velocity can accomplish. Unlike pointy, aerodynamic bullets, round objects build tremendous atmospheric resistance and decelerate quickly. Moreover, the rate of deceleration is proportional to initial velocity, which means the faster a pellet is moving when it leaves the muzzle, the more rapidly it slows down. It also means that down-range energy is virtually the same, pellet for pellet, regardless of muzzle velocity.

If that seems difficult to believe, study the volocity and energy charts in any good loading manual. A No. 6 pellet departing the gun at 1,135 feet per second is traveling 830 fps at twenty yards, 695 fps at forty yards, and 580 fps at sixty yards. Goosing up the muzzle velocity to 1,330 fps produces speeds of 970, 765, and 635 fps at the same ranges. So a velocity differential of 295 fps at the muzzle is only 140 fps at twenty yards and half that at forty yards. The "speed kills" jag that a lot of cartridge makers and shooters are on these days just doesn't make much sense.

Besides, speed never killed anything. Energy is what kills birds and breaks targets, and the same phenomenon that erodes velocity reduces energy as well. Those same two No. 6 pellets, slow and fast, pack 5.55 and 7.62 foot-pounds of energy, respectively, at the muzzle. At twenty yards, it's down to 3.19 and 4.05 foot-pounds; at forty, the punch is 2.08 and 2.52 foot-pounds; and at sixty yards, they're virtually identical: 1.45 and 1.74 foot-pounds. Actually, for all practical purposes they're identical at forty yards; .44 foot-pounds' difference in energy wouldn't be noticed by a canary, much less a cock pheasant.

Clearly, velocity is not the key to killing power. Shot size is the key. The larger the pellet, the greater its mass and the greater, therefore, the energy it can generate.

Is this to say No. 6 is a lousy shot size for pheasants? Not at all. No. 5 can be better under some circumstances, but I would imagine that more pheasants die at the behest of 6s every year than any other size. And the reason they do, the reason why almost all game birds die when you shoot them with shot of any size, is that the effect of pellet energy is cumulative.

Staying with pheasants a moment longer, the best all-around load I know is a charge of hard No. 6 at 1,220 feet per second; any more velocity than that exaggerates the law of diminishing returns. Pellet energy is 3.57 foot-pounds at twenty yards and 2.26 foot-pounds at forty. But sticking a rooster with ten pellets at forty yards is not a matter of hitting him with 2.26 foot-pounds of energy ten times; it's a matter of hitting him with 22.6 foot-pounds once. And that's lethal.

Years ago, somebody made up a table estimating the minimum number of pellets that need to strike the vital areas of various birds in order to ensure a clean kill. Unfortunately, I can no longer lay my hands on it, but such things are of only marginal value anyway. What's important is that reliable kills require multiple hits. We've all had one-pellet-in-the-brain shots that worked out better than they should have, but those are flukes, the exceptions that help prove the rule.

Unlike riflemen who can—theoretically anyway—place their single projectile right where it can have maximum effect, our sort of shooting is necessarily looser, less precise. We can't aim for the heart; all we can do is try to shoot so that we center the pattern on the most vulnerable area of the target. For crossing and quartering shots that's the area from the wings to the head, and right up the wazoo on straightaways.

To complicate things further, concentrating too hard on "centering" any moving object is almost certain to ensure that you won't. The more you bear down, the more you start measuring—looking back and forth from target to gun—and when you do that, you can count on hitting birds too far back or missing behind altogether. Better to stay loose, look ahead of the target, keep the gun moving, and trust your natural ability to point where your eyes are looking.

So why not use the largest pellets available and thus reduce the number of multiple strikes required? After all, two No. 2 pellets starting at 1,220 fps would impart a total of almost fifteen foot-pounds of energy at forty yards, and that should be enough to deck a pheasant if they strike his vitals.

Or why not go the other way and combine very small shot with extra-full choke and up the number of multiple strikes? A No. 9 pellet at 1,200 fps muzzle velocity carries only .65 foot-pounds energy at forty yards, but thirty of them in a pheasant's lights amounts to 19.5 foot-pounds of impact.

Either extreme will work, provided your gun will produce evenly distributed patterns with large shot (most barrels don't), or provided you're a good enough shot to consistently place a very small pattern spread right where you want it (most shooters aren't).

The optimal solution lies somewhere between, and it's simply to combine three elements: the most open boring appropriate to the distance where you take most of your shots; loads your gun will turn into the most evenly-spread patterns with minimum stringing; and the smallest pellets that carry enough energy to deliver a killing blow to whatever bird you're hunting with five or six strikes. The wider your pattern, the greater your margin of error in pointing the gun; the more even the spread and shorter the string, the more efficient the pattern; and the more pellets, the denser the shot swarm.

In finding just the right compromise between pellet weight and pattern density, it's wise to consider the bird. Geese and the larger ducks typically require serious hammering, and large, heavy shot is a must. Pheasants can be remarkably tough and are extremely tenacious of life; they can absorb an astonishing amount of energy and still live long enough to escape. I shoot lots of them with No. 7½ and sometimes even No. 8, but for all-around pheasant hunting, 6s and 5s are better. Doves and quail and woodcock don't require as much shocking power, but their small size puts a premium on pattern density. With the possible exception of sage hens, North American grouse succumb readily to just a moderate blow, and here again, pattern spread and density are considerably more important than big, high-energy pellets.

Although it's possible to achieve the ideal combination of load, pellets, and gun, the onus is still on the shooter. The best loads in the world aren't worth a damn unless you put the shot where the bird is, and do it under circumstances when your chance of success is the highest. Anybody who isn't troubled by the sight of a disappearing bird that's obviously been hit has a gizzard where his heart should be. It happens to everyone sooner or later, despite the best of intentions, but that doesn't make it any easier.

What bothers me as much are the people who insist upon shooting at every bird in sight. It seems to happen most often with pheasants, probably because pheasants are usually the spookiest flushers and are big enough to appear closer than they are. These antics are usually performed by people who couldn't hit an outhouse if you locked them inside, but however lousy their shooting, I have to believe that a few of those pellets find their mark—certainly not enough to put any birds in the bag and usually not enough to make the hits apparent, but still I wonder how many fly off apparently unscathed only to die a lingering death. It doesn't seem right to treat a bird so cavalierly.

It can happen even when the likelihood of a clean kill is all but optimal, and in some ways that's spookiest of all. Last October I hunted grouse in Minnesota, as I always do, and one afternoon we were working back through an old pasture grown up in hazelbrush, nearing the truck. I was on the far right edge, without a dog in front of me, and just as I reached the corner where the brush gives way to a few yards of grass at the road, I put up a grouse.

The bird was under a little leafless bush at the base of a tree, and I saw it just an instant before it flushed. If you've hunted grouse very much, you know the situation: Everything shifts to slow motion except your mind, and you and the bird go into a brief gavotte that feels like being trapped in a dream. I saw it leap, heard its wings, started the little 28-gauge moving even as I stepped sideways away from the bush in front of me. The bird climbed and climbed, right along the cover of the tree trunk; the gun kept coming up and up, and I'm thinking, "Get clear of the tree, get clear of the tree, six more feet, get clear of the tree."

And of course it got clear of the tree, climbing left, and then, as always, everything switched from slo-mo to hyper-drive, and I pulled the trigger while the barrels were still a foot behind a tail that was gone in a blink. It was not the first wasted shot that day. A few flickers through the brush told me the bird was driving west, right down the front of the brush, going strong.

A minute later, I hooked up with Ted in the grassy margin and told him the flight line. We agreed it went one of two ways—down the brush parallel to the road and into the corner where the swampy creek bottom divides the woods from a pasture, or across the road and into a little patch of open woods on the other side. Grouse being grouse, those were the only real options.

So we walked the brush while Beans, Ted's young shorthair, snuffled and scoured ahead of us. Nothing.

We crossed the fence and the road and waded into thigh-deep ferns on the other side and worked that up to field edge. Still nothing. The ferns were easily thick enough to hide in, and we only made one pass, but yet I couldn't quite feature a grouse, once-flushed and therefore edgy, sitting still with two men and a dog tramping anywhere nearby. The only logical answer was that it went west and then cut south, deeper into the woods.

Logic, however, proved inadequate, as it often does with grouse. As we neared Ted's truck, parked on bare ground at the edge of a cut cornfield, Beans suddenly sprinted ahead and picked up a very dead bird lying splay-winged in the open dust.

We put the scenario together on the ride home. I was swinging the gun fast enough to put the leading edge of the pattern farther forward than I thought, just enough that one No. 8 pellet drilled through the flank and into its heart. It was in fact heading for the rather unlikely escape cover across the road (which is good to know about the brush-corner birds in that covert) when its heart gave out. The spread wings said it wasn't yet dead when it finally fell.

And this gave me something to think about. That bird showed absolutely no sign of being hit. Another thirty yards and it would've made the fern-choked understory. If we'd looked long enough, Beans would've found it, but we had no reason to look there for a bird we had no reason to think was dead. Some fox or coyote would have dined well that night.

As it was, I dined well a few nights later, on a perfectly roasted grouse set off by a bottle of really good California Merlot. And offered a silent toast, one of respectful regrets to a long-dead pheasant, and to the red gods, for soothing my soul yet one more time.

23

ROLLING
YOUR OWN
GAME LOADS

For about thirty years now, I've spent the better part of each August at my loading bench, cranking out a season's worth of cartridges for the hunting I have planned during the fall and winter. Besides making me feel like a properly industrious ant rather than a frivolous grasshopper, the project also helps occupy a portion of the year that's too hot, too long, and too close to hunting season to be bearable without some distraction.

Actually, I used to spend a good portion of about eight other months pulling the handles of my faithful old MEC loaders, shucking off target shells by the zillion in support of an addiction to hurling swarms of lead shot at flying discs of graphite and pitch. I don't shoot as many targets as I used to, but even when I did, the preseason loading was always different. Target shells were donkey work governed by the precepts of Never Discard a Hull Till Not Even Candle Wax or Duct

Tape Will Keep the Crimp Closed, and Get 'Em Loaded and Boxed and Let's Go Shoot. It was time grudgingly spent, and I always envied the guys who could afford hydraulic loaders that ran at the speed of sewing machines.

Making game cartridges, on the other hand, is an exercise in serenity and precision, performed to quiet music on the shop radio with a glass of Merlot standing by, my head wreathed in fragrant pipesmoke as I assemble the shells and mark each box with the load, the gun, and the birds they're meant for.

(I know that component manufacturers and publishers of loading data all caution against drinking and smoking while loading ammunition. It's not something I recommend, just something I sometimes do. If your tolerance is such that you get fuzzy-headed from one glass of wine, you should avoid it while operating anything more complicated than a crayon or toilet paper. As to smoking, nitrocellulose powder is relatively difficult to ignite. You can do it with a cigarette, but it would require a pretty weird accident with a pipe. If you want a real thrill, lay your pipe on the bench while you're tying flies, let a stray wisp of marabou fall into the bowl, and then relight it without looking. Or go smoke an old down vest. I imagine it tastes about the same.)

Anyway, I love loading game cartridges. In some ways it represents a way of paying respects to my guns and to the birds I hope to find. You could argue that not even the most carefully assembled handloads will be any better than the best factory-loaded shells you can buy, or that the money you save by rolling your own is offset by the time you spend doing it, and I could only say that you're right on all counts, but I like it anyway.

For one thing, handloading allows you to shoot the kind of loads that make sense to you, rather than just having to accept what the manufacturers think the majority of shooters wants or needs. It wasn't so long ago that you couldn't get a factory-made ⅞-ounce 12-gauge cartridge or a ¾-ounce 20 for love nor money. It was hard enough to buy a decent one-ounce 12-bore load. Anybody who understood how wonderfully deadly light loads can be was S.O.L. if he didn't load his own and even

stress on a gun, depending. And if it's a gun you're inclined to coddle, pressure is something to take into account. Your choice of powder generally influences this more than anything else. The slower the burning rate, the lower the pressure. Most of the DuPont recipes for mild loads, for instance, call for SR7625, which has been my favorite low-pressure powder for about twenty-five years. Regardless of who makes them, slow-burning powders are adaptable to a wide variety of cases, primers, and wads.

On the other hand, if achieving low pressure isn't a great concern but cleanliness is, you can tailor your game loads that way, too. The slow-burning powders tend to leave a lot of gunk in the bore, which is why your smallbore guns get so dirty from shooting factory shells. Faster-burning propellants are cleaner. If you're going to fire a lot of shells—say, at doves—in a relatively new gun, it's not a bad idea to think in terms of keeping your barrels clean, for more consistent ballistics. That's a good reason to choose powders like DuPont Hi-Skor 700-X, Red Dot, Hodgdon Clays, or Winchester WST. They burn quickly and don't leave much residue behind.

I mentioned smallbores for a reason. Just a glance at the industry maximum-pressure chart shows that chamber pressure increases as bores get smaller simply because reducing bore diameter increases bearing surface with the shot column, which therefore increases friction and the amount of force necessary to drive the charge down the tube. It's inescapable, and it means that the faster-burning powders are unsuitable for the smallest gauges. Having dirty barrels is the price you pay for shooting 20s and 28s. Choosing recipes for smallbores is a juggling act in finding loads that generate sufficient velocity with relatively minimal pressure.

More and more hunters are using English guns these days, and they present a dual concern: You don't want to exceed the working pressure for which they were proofed, and the typical English game gun is bored for 2½-inch cases. Factory cartridges are available, but they're not always easy to find and not always cheap. Here's one instance where reloading truly is economical, and the loading industry is catching on. Most of the major loading-press manufacturers offer conversion kits to accommodate short cases; specialty companies such as Ballistic Products can supply accessories; and some of the powder companies are starting to publish loading data for short cases. Most notably Hodgdon, whose new manual not only lists recipes for both 2- and 2½-inch 12-bores but also describes how to make them from the most common American 2 ¾-inch cases.

Once you've found a recipe that balances your needs for adequate ballistics against a concern for the welfare of your gun, the rest of the game-load scenario is straightforward and relatively simple.

Pure lead is fine for informal target shooting, but it's too soft to deliver either the best patterns or optimal killing power on game, and if you're going to pull the trigger on a game bird, you'll want it to die quickly and cleanly. That means hard shot, alloyed with antimony. Plating alone, either with copper or nickel, is not a substitute for hardness. Hard shot is more expensive, but it's the only thing to use.

So are once-fired hulls. If you reload to shoot targets for fun, the life of a cartridge case is essentially however long it remains in one piece and stiff enough at the mouth to hold its crimp, with or without some first aid. But after one or two firings, even the best plastic hulls start to lose their crispness, and a tight crimp is important to ballistic consistency. As their physical properties decline, so does the ballistics they deliver, and erratic performance is not what you're looking for in game loads.

It should go without saying, but unfortunately often doesn't that once you've chosen a recipe you should follow it to the letter. Changing powder or shot charges, substituting components, and generally tinkering with a recipe is stepping into the unknown, and the surprises you find are seldom good. Merely swapping one brand of primer for another can significantly raise pressures, and so, of course, can dumping in an extra grain or two of powder. Swapping wads can turn a good load all but useless.

Having gone the route, my best advice is that not every factory shell you fire is a good candidate for reloading. They all can be reloaded, of course, but it's a question of economics. Thirty years ago I was a college instructor working under a contract for a five-figure annual income, and because the amount of shooting I got to do was directly proportional to how little it cost, I hoarded hulls as if they were gold and reloaded every one. Eventually, I accumulated enough components to stock a gun shop—primers, powder, and wads for every type of hull I had. The problem was that I had only a hundred or fewer of certain hulls, and when they wore out, the components were useless unless I went off looking for more of those hulls, whether I liked them or not. The whole thing was penny-wise and pound-foolish, to say nothing of the time I spent readjusting the powder measure and perhaps the shot measure as well (I've always preferred a calibrated charge bar to bushings) and resetting the drop tube to seat the wads—all to load no more than three or four boxes of shells.

Since then I've reduced the whole thing to one or two brands of hulls, using only two or three favorite recipes each. It's simplified the variety of components I need and reduced the time I have to spend setting up. This is good, even in those preseason weeks when loading is a labor of love, because it means less time dinking around and more time actually building the cartridges and thinking about where we'll be going together when the cool days finally come.

MAXIMUM CHAMBER PRESSURES

as established by the Sporting Arms and Ammunition Manufacturers Institute

Gauge & Case	Pressure
10	11,000 psi
12, 3½"	14,000 psi
12, 3"	11,500 psi
12, 2¾"	11,500 psi
16	11,500 psi
20, 3"	12,000 psi
20, 2¾"	12,000 psi
28	12,500 psi
.410, 3"	13,500 psi
.410, 2½"	12,500 psi

CONTROVERSIES

24

SHOOTING
IN THE ZONE

It was hard to tell just how large the flock really was, partly because they were screened by the alder scrub and partly because even halfway through the change from reddish summer plumage to snowy-white winter dress a ptarmigan can blend remarkably well into the mottled textures of an old volcanic ash-bed. On the Alaska Peninsula, early October is a moment on the cusp between vastly different worlds, and the birds were in transition not only between color phases but also from their summertime family groups to the huge flocks they form in winter. For two days we'd found them in little knots of a half-dozen, in twenty- or thirty-bird packs, in flocks of a hundred or more.

This clearly was one of the larger congregations and therefore likely to produce some impressive film footage. As it was my turn onstage, I waited until Joe gave the signal and then

MORE SHOTGUNS AND SHOOTING

moved in. From where we'd first spotted them it was easily a forty-bird affair; at thirty yards there were twice that many. When they flushed at twenty yards the number doubled yet again, into a blizzard of hammering wings and hurtling bodies rising in close order from right to left, stark against the sky. It was, as they say, picture perfect.

I swung the gun, triggered one shot, then a second, turned to look down the bore of Joe's softly humming camera, and said, "Now there we have a good example of damn poor shooting."

"That flush was spectacular," Joe said, lowering his infernal machine. "Filled the frame. We'll leave that one in."

Oh, wonderful. Out of nearly two hundred specimens of a bird that is not difficult to hit, all rising in full view at less than a hundred feet, I manage to bag a total of absolutely nothing, have the whole thing captured on video tape, and Mr. Director is going to leave it in.

But I suppose you could argue that being an example of what not to do is better than being no example at all, and there really is a lesson in it. That wasn't the first time I've fired into a skyful of birds and failed to cut a feather, and I'm sure it won't be the last. I've done the same thing with quail and doves, gray partridge and driven pheasants, even clay targets. I'll bet you've done it, too, so you know how it feels to stand there like a bozo while birds that ought to be dead go off to fly another day.

There's a perfectly simple reason why it happens. It's all in our heads, more specifically our eyes. In the case of the ptarmigan I was looking at all of them, not at any particular bird, and my shot charges went right where I was looking—which is to say, nowhere in particular. The same thing happens when you look at a covey of quail rather than one quail. Swing on two clay targets traveling more or less together, try to watch them both at the same time, and you'll shoot right between them.

It is axiomatic that a shot charge goes where your eyes go, assuming you have a gun that fits reasonably well and that you handle it reasonably well. Or even if you don't, at least to some extent. Both gun fit and technique offer fairly broad margins of error; if they didn't, few of us could hit much of anything with out-of-the-box factory guns nor accommodate all the variables of field shooting.

Eyes are different. Eyes are our connection with the target, act as the conduit for the shots we fire. As in horseshoes, "close" counts in shooting but only just. You can have the best-fitted gun there is and handle it flawlessly, and still miss shot after shot if your eyes aren't taking your hands to the target.

And it's not just a matter of picking a bird and keeping your eyes on it. It's a matter of focus, in two senses of the word. Your optical system has to resolve a fairly clear image of a moving object if it's to guide your hands with any degree of accuracy. Let's assume the equipment works as it should, either unassisted or with aid of the optometrist's art.

Focus is also concentration, and that's where the act of shooting most often breaks down. It would be nice to have enough visual acuity to determine the sex of a gnat at fifty paces, but the lack of it is no real handicap. Plain old 20/20, or even 20/40, is good enough, provided you use it.

The fact is, we are lazy lookers. I don't know exactly what proportion of our potential acuity we really use in the course of everyday life, but I know it isn't nearly as much as we really have. We usually don't need it all. A glance is enough to fix the position of a bite of food or an oncoming automobile, to scan a paragraph of print or a television screen. Trust me, though: If you merely glance at a game bird or a clay target, you might as well save the cartridge. I've glanced at a lot of them, and hardly a one ever came to any subsequent grief.

We all can see better than we realize, and it takes surprisingly little effort to make remarkable things happen.

Among the current generation of top-notch shooting instructors, Dan Carlisle probably places more emphasis on visual concentration than anyone, and he uses a highly effective little trick to open the door on this with new students. Some clay targets in hand, he backs off twenty feet or so and asks you to watch. He throws one straight up, with the dome facing you; you follow it to its apogee and then back down to the ground. Piece of cake. Then he throws another and asks if you saw anything different. In a group lesson, usually only about half notice that he's felt-tipped a black dot the size of a dime right in the center of the second one. When the third one goes up and everyone knows what to look at, that same tiny black spot looks as big as a golfball and the target itself seems the size of a Frisbee.

Two important points to be taken here: One is that normal, average human vision is capable of more high-resolution acuity than most of us know. Counting the stitches on a fastball requires an exceptional set of eyes, but with a little practice and concentration just about everyone can see that it has stitches, and that's far more acuity than we customarily bring to bear.

The other point is that focusing on a small part of some object makes the whole thing appear larger. If you want to test this right now, look across the room at a bookcase and read some titles. Then look again, but don't just read; look to see if the type they're printed in has serifs. If it does and you can see them, the letters will suddenly seem twice the size they did before.

Apply this to a moving object and it will not only appear larger but also slower. It happens through a combination of visual and mental concentration. I know a couple of professional race-car drivers, highly rated competitors in the sport, and both have described to me the phenomenon they call "making the track slow down." What they mean is that when they concentrate their eyes and minds within a certain range of track ahead, everything shifts to a sort of slow motion. They are in fact making split-second responses at 180 miles per hour, but they can do so with unhurried precision and great physical economy.

The same thing applies to shooting, though in a somewhat different way. A driver has to keep his focus over the whole course of a race; a gunner needs to do it only for a few seconds on each shot. Every moving target, feathered or clay, is in view and in range for a finite period of time. Within that is a sub-period I think of as the zone of focus (I'm not very good at coining buzzwords, so this could be someone else's phrase that I've picked up without realizing it; if it is, my apologies).

The zone of focus is that frame in space and time when a clay target ceases to be an orange streak in the air and visually becomes a clay target—a domed disc with sharply stepped edges, dimples, and a logo. It's the same span in which a bird changes from a fluttery shape to a real animal complete with head, body, wings, tail, feet, eyes, feathers, and all the rest. The more sharply you see the details, the more slowly it seems to move.

The moment doesn't last very long in either case, but if your head's in the game it doesn't have to. You'll see all the component parts instead of the whole, and that's the time to react and shoot. React too soon, before your eyes are truly in control, and the shot will be little more than a knee-jerk twitch; if you wait too long, extraneous things will intrude and shatter your concentration.

I doubt there's a hunter alive who can't remember at least a few times when he's been so fully focused on a particular bird that he could even see the shot pellets strike. That's how it was with the first ruffed grouse I ever shot. I saw the bars on its tailfeathers, the white spots on the feathers of its rump and back, the pale streaks and mottles of its neck and shoulders, could even see each twig of the background within a small space around the bird. Everything else was vague and formless, like a vignette photograph; all I had to do was point the gun at that window, and I remember feeling a sense of complete, perfect control without the slightest need to hurry.

Everyone's optimal zone opens at a slightly different time and place. Older eyes don't focus as rapidly as young ones, nor are older reflexes quite as snappy as they used to be—but only when the one accommodates the other is the moment truly right. The difference may be a matter of milliseconds, but they're crucial nonetheless. Your greatest chance of success lives in your zone, wherever it is.

To start building a sense of where that might be, spend some time on a target range while someone else is shooting at crossing or going-away targets. At first focus your eyes close to the trap. If you see anything at all, it will likely be just a little streak; you'll have to chase it with your eyes, and it will remain impossibly small and fast.

Then, in increments of three or four feet at a time, move your focal point out from the trap along the path the target will take, and keep moving out until you find the spot where the streak becomes a target. That's where your zone begins. You can focus on specific parts of any target in it—on the top, the bottom, the leading edge, whatever. For the next few moments the target will be big and bright and clear and slow-moving, and if you point your finger at it you'll find it remarkably easy to touch.

The other guy may be able to see it sooner. Yet another might take half again longer. That's for them to figure out and deal with. You can't shoot well in someone else's zone, only in your own.

It goes with you to the game fields as well, and you can find it the same way. Don't look at the ground in front of the dog in anticipation of the flush; look at the air above the ground, at waist-level or higher, and find the place where your first sight of the bird comes just as it enters the zone.

An oncoming target may seem different because you can see it for a relatively longer time. In fact it isn't so different at all; an oncoming dove, duck, pheasant, or clay simply enters your zone from the far side, and your view of it gets progressively better. Those can be the hardest or the easiest shots of all—hard if you mount the gun too soon and try to ride the bird on its way in, easy if you do nothing but watch until it's in the zone and in perfect focus and then take the shot in one short, smooth motion.

All this is easily said, of course. The fact is, finding the zone takes some conscious effort and a bit of practice, but it really does work. And you don't have to go through an entire round of targets or a full day's hunting continually focused like a shaft of sunlight through a burning-glass. That's exhausting, and unnecessary besides. The trick is in developing the ability to switch your concentration on when you really need it and save your energy when you don't. World-class target and pigeon shots have this refined to a high level, and it's one reason why they can perform the way they do.

The rest of us won't be so consistent, but that's okay. Momentary lapses aren't the end of the world. We all take little mental vacations while shooting now and then. Yours probably won't end up immortalized on film, and most of mine don't either. The vagaries of Alaskan weather brought our video project to a premature halt that somehow never got restarted. I'm sorry I never got to go back to that particular place for more ptarmigan and some Sandy River steelhead, but not sorry that a certain piece of tape is still in a can somewhere out of sight. Anyone who's ever seen me shoot knows what a doofus I can be with a gun sometimes, without having the evidence available for instant replay. I'd just as soon keep it that way.

25

Out of
a Slump

Funny word, slump, especially if you repeat it a few times. Slump. Sounds like a pig falling out of bed. But combine it with an adjective and it's not so funny: batting slump, free-throw slump, putting slump. Shooting slump.

One of the oddest things about having the ability to perform a complex physical act is that it occasionally disappears, suddenly, unaccountably, and, as it sometimes seems, permanently. Doesn't matter what tool you use—golf club, tennis racket, pool cue, shotgun—you can be a demon one day and a dud the next, and the next, and the next.

A slump is not just a bad day. It's a whole bunch of bad days strung together, and it can last for a week or a month or even longer. It can also take on epic proportions. Possibly the most spectacular display of misperformance I ever saw was the day one of my friends, about two weeks into a dreadful shooting slump, fired exactly seventy-five shells to collect exactly one dove.

Now it's one thing if he'd been a lousy shot to begin with, but he wasn't. He was in fact a very good shot, and therein lies the nature of the slump. Poor shots don't have slumps; poor shots have just the opposite, occasional brief periods when they shoot fairly well. A real slump presupposes a relatively high level of ability.

So, it is perverse and mystifying when a well-tuned skill abruptly departs, and damnably frustrating. I know; I've been there, more than once, and so have all my shooting partners. You probably have, too, and like everyone else, wondered how we get into these things and, even more to the point, how to get out.

A slump is cause and effect. It's not that you've really lost your ability, though it often feels that way, but rather that something is interfering with your ability.

It could be your gun, especially if you've recently switched guns. The worst slump I ever went through coincided precisely with the three years in the early 1970s when I owned, and was determined to shoot, a certain 16-bore Parker, a nice little VH Grade with 26-inch barrels and factory single trigger. Being at the time thoroughly marinated in the Parker mystique, I thought it was the be-all and end-all of guns. What it was, in fact, was a disaster.

There wasn't anything wrong with it as a gun, but there was plenty wrong with it as *my* gun. The stock was way too short and had too much drop; the balance was tipped too far back, which made the business end jittery as the dickens; and it was choked tighter than an owl's butt. I knew all that, but I was so taken with the idea of shooting a Parker that I refused to even think it might not be the right gun for me.

I've never shot so poorly for so long. It was okay at clay targets, but a bird in the air was about 98 percent safe. No matter how hard I tried, I just could not hit much of anything. I owned guns that fit me better and handled better, but after a couple of years fooling with that damn Parker I couldn't hit much of anything with them, either. Finally, I gave up and sold it, but even at that it took almost another year to relearn how to shoot.

It taught me two things. One is that it's utter folly to try fitting yourself to a gun rather than the other way around. The other is that the sheer frustration of being in a slump is oftentimes the very thing that keeps you in it.

In order to go from competent shot to duffer almost overnight, something has to change, and if it's not the gun, it has to be you. I've worked for years and years on developing a concise, consistent, effective technique of handling a shotgun. I don't hit everything I shoot at, nobody does, but when I handle the gun properly, something usually breaks or dies and if it doesn't, time after time, then I know I'm making some error in technique. It might be very small, so subtle that I don't recognize it right away, but it's there, and it usually involves something fundamental, some little bad habit that's crept into my shooting and stuck long enough to become a big bad habit.

In large part, good shooting is an act of faith, a willingness to trust our natural eye-hand coordination, and that's the basis of a sound technique: Keep your head dead-still, raise the gun to your cheek and point it like pointing a finger, go after the target with your forward hand first, swing, mount and fire all in one motion, relying on the fact that you'll point the gun right where your eyes are looking.

When we try to be too precise, too deliberate, and think too much, we end up outsmarting our own ability. Unfortunately, frustration just makes it worse, turns small errors into big ones. The more we miss, the more we bear down, slam the gun butt to the shoulder, drop the head to the stock, aim it like a rifle, look back and forth from barrel to target, try to drill it absolutely dead-center and end up missing by a mile. Lose your technique and you've lost your shot.

Speed is a factor, too. Every experienced shot develops his own speed in handling a gun. It may be quick or slow, but it's his pace and if he departs from it very much, he'll start missing. Here again, the frustration of a slump plays the spoiler.

The first tendency is to rush, to get off a shot before the bird escapes. When you do that, your technique doesn't have time to come together; you poke at the bird instead of swinging on it. Then, chances are you'll try to be ultra-deliberate, but if you slow down too much, you'll start measuring, start looking from bird to barrel, and every time you look at the barrel you stop moving it. Lose your timing and you've lost your shot.

So what's the cure? How do you get out of the hole you've dug for yourself?

One of the best ways is to just take a break. Don't shoot for a week or two. Give yourself time to forget the frustration, to stop trying to think the whole thing to death, and fall back on the technique you've learned. Ever notice how often you do really well at something you haven't done for a while, like golf or tennis or pool, how natural and easy it seems when you first take it up again? It works that way because you simply let your hands and eyes work together without trying to second-guess what you can do naturally. It's the same with shooting.

Sometimes you can shoot your way out of a slump, but you have to change the circumstances. To a hunter, how he shoots at game is what's most important, so if you start missing birds you might be able to work it out on targets. Clay targets don't mean much. So what if you miss one, or ten? There are a zillion more where they came from. It can take the pressure off, let you relax.

Better yet, have a shooting lesson. A good instructor can readily spot problems of technique that might take days to figure out for yourself. That's why big-time athletes like golfers and tennis players have trainers.

And sometimes you can solve a slump by changing guns. The one you're using might fit you perfectly, but if you shoot a lot, you can become so accustomed to the feel of it that you lose some awareness of how you're handling it, and that can be a ticket to sloppy technique. Switching to a lighter or heavier gun—one that also fits you well, of course—can make a big difference; just being aware of what's in your hands can help you concentrate on how you use it.

Prevention is the best cure of all. As I said before, one bad day is not a slump, but it can be the beginning of one, and if you can nip it in the bud, you won't have to deal with it in full bloom. Everyone has off-days, and for all sorts of reasons. When I have one I try to figure out why. What kind of shots did I have—reasonable opportunities or very difficult ones? You can't expect to hit as many hard shots as easy ones. Was it just one of those days when I was mostly in the wrong place at the wrong time? That happens. Was it a long, tiring day, and did my shooting get worse as I grew wearier? To be expected.

Was I having trouble seeing the birds, because of poor light or confusing backgrounds or a smudged contact lens? You can't hit what you can't see, at least not consistently. Did my eye dominance change? I'm right-handed and pretty strongly right-eyed, but once in a while, fatigue makes my left eye start to take over. When that happens, I smear a bit of Chapstick on the left lens of my shooting glasses; it helps, but I still don't shoot as well as usual.

If there's a reasonable explanation for having an off-day, don't fret about it. Next time is likely to be different. But if I can only conclude that I just shot poorly, then it's time to do a bit of work on the basics and run through some fifteen- or twenty-minute drills of swing, mount and dry-fire. If I'm going hunting again in the next day or two, I'll take a different gun. If I'm not, it's off to the gun club for some skeet or sporting clays.

Mercifully, I haven't suffered a real slump in quite a while—mostly, I suspect, because I've taken great pains not to let one get started. Bird seasons are too short to mar with frustration, and life's too short not to treat every season as if it might be my last.

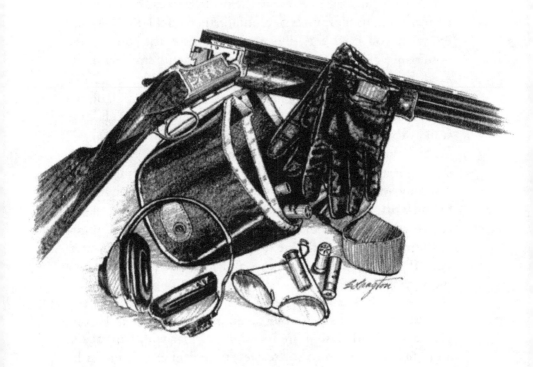

26

SHOOTING

AND HEARING

A Comedy in One Act: THE
SCENE: Copper Creek Farm, in the Missouri Ozarks. TIME:
Early summer, 1997.

VICKY enters through the mudroom door, carrying
shopping bags.

VICKY. Hellooo.

MICHAEL. (From his office down the hallway.) Hi, sweetie.
Have a good time?

VICKY. (Going into the kitchen.) Yeah. The traffic's awful,
so I didn't get all my errands done. I got you a present, though.

MICHAEL. You did? What is it?

VICKY. A movie.

MICHAEL. Which one?

VICKY. .... (The words are slightly obscured by the rustle
of bags and other sounds as she moves about the kitchen.)

(MICHAEL leaves his office, walks down the hallway, through the mudroom, and enters the kitchen, a puzzled look on his face.)

MICHAEL. Why in the world did you buy that?

VICKY. It's one of your favorites, isn't it?

MICHAEL. *Brain Parts*? I never heard of it.

VICKY. (Puzzled, too.) *Brain Parts*? What are you talking about?

MICHAEL. You said you bought *Brain Parts*.

VICKY. I said I bought *Braveheart*. (Laughing.) *Brain Parts*! Sweetie, you need a hearing aid.

THE END

This kind of thing happens all the time, although the discrepancies between what people say to me and what I think I hear don't usually become family jokes the way this one has. I'm glad to be amusing, but the fact is, I'm hard of hearing and I got that way from shooting.

Everybody knows gunfire is loud. Some know that if you listen to it long enough, it'll damage your hearing. But too few shooters seem to understand just how loud it is or how insidious the effect can be.

Sound is typically measured for two qualities—loudness and pitch. Loudness is expressed in decibels, abbreviated dB. A single decibel is the least difference in sound intensity that the human ear can distinguish. The scale ranges from 0 dB, which is the faintest we can detect, to more than 180 dB—the noise level of a space rocket leaving its launching pad.

Pitch is the frequency of sound vibrations in cycles per second, expressed in hertz units, or Hz. One Hz equals one cycle per second. Humans normally can hear sounds pitched from about 20 Hz to about 20,000 Hz—from the lowest note of a pipe organ to the high pitch of a so-called silent dog whistle, which some people can hear. Other animals are capable of detecting sounds over a much broader range.

In the human hearing apparatus, sound waves are gathered by the outer ear and channeled through the ear canal to the eardrum. Behind the eardrum, in the middle ear, three tiny bones—the hammer, anvil, and stirrup—transfer vibrations from the eardrum to the inner ear. There, in a coiled structure called the cochlea, the vibrations are translated to electrical impulses by hairlike cells connected to minute nerve endings. These combine to form the auditory nerve, which carries the impulses to the brain. The brain, in turn, interprets these as sound.

It's a wonderful system but quite delicate, especially in the inner ear, and sounds that exceed a certain level of loudness can physically damage it.

To understand how intense sound can be, it's useful to know that the decibel scale is logarithmic and increases by factors of ten. A 10 dB sound is ten times louder than one of 0 dB, 20 dB is ten times louder than 10 dB, 30 dB a hundred times louder, and so on. At 80 dB, which is about the noise level of very heavy traffic, sound is 100 million times more intense than the softest sound we can hear.

From 90 to 110 dB—from a lawn mower to a motorcycle—sound waves start to batter the hairlike cells in the cochlea, and from 120 dB on, the shock begins to kill the nerves they're attached to. At 130 dB, sound becomes so intense that we can feel as well as hear it, and at 140 dB, about the level of a jet plane on takeoff, noise becomes intensely painful.

So where does gunfire fit into this?

A typical 12-gauge target load delivers a muzzle blast of about 130 dB. That's ten trillion times louder than our threshold of hearing. And it's enough to destroy your hearing—not all at once, usually, but gradually, shot by shot, year by year.

As the tiny nervelets in the inner ear die off, the auditory nerve becomes less and less able to carry information to the brain. Think of it as a lamp cord made of a bundle of tiny wires; start taking wires away strand by strand, and eventually there won't be enough of them left to carry enough juice to light the bulb. Typically, this happens on a cycle of damage and recovery. After a few rounds of skeet or trap, or having your chimes rung by your hunting partner's gun, you notice a buzz in your ears, maybe even a slight headache. It lasts a few days and then goes away, until next time. The problem is, each recovery is less than the one before, two steps forward after three steps back.

Eventually, you begin to notice that high-frequency sound is rather murky, even slightly garbled. The impairment works its way down the frequency scale and eventually gets into the range of speech, which is from 3,000 Hz to 500 Hz. Then, the more background noise there is, the more difficult it is to hear a conversation. Higher-pitched voices are especially hard to hear clearly, even at close range. You can hear the sound but can't make out the words.

You're going deaf. Noise-induced hearing loss is hearing loss from nerve damage, and nerve damage is irreversible. Even the symptoms are difficult to treat. Because it amplifies everything, the standard sort of hearing aid is no help at all. Only the latest, high-tech aids capable of amplifying speech-range frequencies while filtering background noise will do any good, but even then the benefits are limited. Going deaf from nerve damage is not like losing your visual acuity. In most cases, glasses or contact lenses can restore your vision to 20/20; lose your hearing to noise exposure and nothing will ever bring it back.

Is that scary enough? Does it make you want to be sure you're wearing some kind of ear protection when you shoot?

Well, I'll tell you something even scarier.

I've worn ear protection faithfully for thirty years, always when shooting targets, often when hunting—and I've still gone about half deaf.

Years ago, neither the variety nor the quality of ear-protecting devices amounted to much. Nobody wore any kind of protection while hunting, and wads of cotton were the target shooter's standby. Cotton is useless; you can stuff your ears full of it and still only reduce the intensity of sound by six or seven decibels. That's not enough, but it's about all we had.

In the late 1960s, I started using what then amounted to state-of-the-art protection for shooters—fluted, soft rubber plugs enclosing little aluminum cylinders with openings at each end and spring-loaded pistons inside. I loved 'em. I could wear them and still hear normal speech. Theoretically, loud noises physically cause the tiny pistons to seal the openings and block the sound.

Apparently they do block some of the noise, maybe even most of it. But they don't get it all, and what got through eventually got me. It took a long time and who knows how many tens of thousands of shots, but by the late '80s I had a classic case of what the audiologists call "shooter's ear." About 60 percent of the high-frequency hearing in my left ear was gone. Not impaired, gone. My right ear was only about half as bad, thanks to head-shadow. Depending on which shoulder you shoot from, your head blocks some of the noise from getting to the ear that's next to the stock.

This uneven loss is what distinguishes shooter's ear from the deafness caused by working around loud machinery and such, and if there's any sort of hidden blessing it's only that we don't go quite as deaf as we might otherwise.

Which is thin comfort. I have a terrible time hearing conversation in crowded restaurants or at cocktail parties. I can hear voices just fine, but unless I concentrate and use my right ear, you might as well be speaking in Urdu or some obscure dialect of Chinese for all I can distinguish the words you say. Women's voices are more difficult for me than men's, and the piping tones of small children are impossible. I have an amplifier on my telephone, and I need it more often than not.

Once I realized just how much hearing I'd lost, I naturally took a serious interest in preventing it from getting any worse and have since made a point of keeping track of the latest advances in hearing protection for shooters. And I'm happy to say, there are some really good devices available.

I've never liked wearing earmuffs. They're hot, I don't like having anything clamped around my head, and I find the click of my gunstock against them thoroughly annoying. But that's not to say there aren't good muffs on the market. When properly worn, standard muffs attenuate sound by about 25 dB, and some of the new, fluid-filled muffs do even better. Just be aware that anything between the ear pad and your head—be it the temples of your glasses, your cap, or even your hair—reduces their effectiveness.

Semi-aurals, which are little rubber plugs on a flexible headband, are okay, but they don't fit far enough into your ear to be very effective over the long term.

Plugs that go fully into the ear canal are best of all. Simple foam plugs, the kind you compress and then allow to expand in your ear canals, do a remarkably good job, reducing noise intensity as much as 35 dB. You can reduce it another 5 to 10 dB by wearing foam plugs and earmuffs in combination.

If filling the ear canal is the key, then filling it completely is clearly the ideal, and as good as foam plugs are for that, nothing works better than custom-molded plugs. These, which are made by packing your ears with a soft, plastic material that's allowed to harden in place, are the ultimate means of accommodating the exact shape of your ear canals. Properly done, the resulting plugs are durable, comfortable, and do a superb job of attenuating sound. You can get good custom-molded plugs from a number of sources, but Electronic Shooters Protection, Inc. (known as ESP, 11997 West 85th Place, Arvada, Colorado 80005-5138, phone 800-767-7791) takes it a step further by filling the plugs with copper-plated shot. These not only block sound, but the shot effectively shatters loud noise so that what gets through is merely a whisper of its former self.

Protection devices that rely solely upon their physical presence have one drawback: They block all sounds, not just loud ones. Conversation is difficult, and walking while wearing solid, molded plugs sets up all sorts of weird crackles and pops that seem to come from inside your head. Some shooters find all this annoying, and I suspect it's one of the main reasons why many don't wear them.

ESP has solved this problem brilliantly, to my mind, by incorporating sophisticated electronic circuitry. Each custom-molded plug is fitted with a tiny unit, driven by a hearing-aid battery, that suppresses loud noises and at the same time amplifies low-volume, low-frequency sound. This means you can hear your partners, dog bells, target traps springing, and the whir of flushing wings and still receive maximum protection from the impact of gunfire. Each plug has its own volume-control dial, which is particularly nice for those of us who suffer the imbalanced hearing acuity of shooter's ear. I've worn ESP electronic plugs for several years now while teaching, shooting targets and hunting, and according to my most recent hearing test, I've had no additional hearing loss in that time. I really can't imagine a better system.

The official party line of the shooting industry, adopted by all the organizations that govern the shooting sports, is something like "Thou shalt wear hearing protection every time thou firest ye gun." This is an excellent policy, but I don't strictly follow it and I suspect that a lot of others don't, either. Just as the reality of environmental protection is based upon maintaining acceptable levels of degradation, the most realistic question of hearing protection for shooters often hinges upon minimizing loss rather than preventing it altogether.

Shooters with congenital hearing problems obviously should protect themselves any time they have a gun in their hands, but for the rest of us, it's more often a matter of choosing to do so only when the risk is highest. Any sort of target shooting is a high-risk situation; not only do you fire a lot of shots over a short time, but you're also exposed to noise from other shooters. Shoot a round of skeet with four partners and you'll be subjected to twenty-five blasts of your own and a hundred more from the others. Same with trap. A round of sporting clays may involve anywhere from two to four times more shots. My policy now is to wear earplugs any time I'm at a target range, regardless of whether I'm shooting or just watching, and during any session at the patterning plate.

I also wear them for game shooting when there are lots of shots fired and other guns nearby, like driven birds and doves. I wear them in a duck blind, too, if anyone's in there with me.

I don't often wear them for upland hunting, where shots are relatively few and my companions usually some distance away. Hunting grouse and woodcock and quail in thick cover,

I want to be able to hear my partners and the dogs and the birds. The ESP electronic plugs allow me to do that, but I can't seem to locate the direction of sound quite as well as I can with the naked ear.

Still, I've made a pact with myself that I'll start wearing them all the time whenever my annual hearing test shows any noticeable further loss, and I'm sure it'll happen eventually. Meanwhile, I'll go on protecting myself against high-risk shooting, power tools, and other noisy things and try not to appear an utter dolt when I'm unable to hear more than three words in ten during a conversation. And of course, keep the volume up while watching my favorite movie, *Brain Parts*.

27

PRESEASON
TUNEUP

Hang around any gun club during the last weekends of summer, and you'll see an annual phenomenon taking place, predictable as a salmon run or the migration of ducks. A whole procession of guys show up wearing hunting vests and carrying bird guns, shoot one or two rounds of trap or skeet, and depart, not to be seen there again for twelve months.

It's their annual pilgrimage to acquit one of the obligations of the faith, as expressed in the commandment: Thou shalt tune up thy Shooting prior to ye Bird Season. Unfortunately, what they're really going to do is spend about half the coming season relearning how to shoot, and in the process make what should be the best days of the year an exercise in frustration.

For a bird hunter, the question isn't why get your shooting in good form before the season opens; the question is how to make the most of the practice you do, and how much is enough?

The short answer is that there's no such thing as too much. The two boxes of shells that a lot of hunters consider adequate is about one-tenth of what you should plan to shoot if you want to be truly on your gun by opening day. A case of cartridges in the course of a month—and I mean a real case of 500, not the ten-box flats that most ammunition makers are calling "cases" these days—is the minimum for getting the feel of your gun and putting a good edge on your technique.

Unless you have ready access to a couple of feedlots full of feral pigeons and starlings, both of which are sporty enough to be worth any bird hunter's attention, that much shooting means clay targets.

Targets can be excellent practice for bird hunting or largely a waste of time. It all depends upon how you go about it and how selective, or at times creative, you are in setting up the shots that'll really do some good. But once you find those shots, you can repeat them as often as you want, and that's an advantage hard to come by any other way.

You can make it count most of all by combining your actual shooting with some dry-fire exercises.

Effective wingshooting is mainly a matter of tracing flight lines, of moving your gun barrel along the path the bird is taking, and learning to swing through. It's like using your barrel as if it's a pencil with which you draw a line from where the bird just was to where it is to where it's going to be when the shot gets there.

You can do a lot toward developing the ability to visualize flight lines right at home, never firing a shot, with a little drill in swinging your gun along the straight lines that are all around us—the roofline of your house or garage, a tree trunk or a long limb, power lines, the junction of walls and ceiling in a room, and so on.

Imagine that a bird is going to fly right along one of these lines and that you're going to kill him about two-thirds of the way across; swing and mount, keeping the muzzle on the line from the time you start the gun moving till a moment after you pull the trigger. You can change the angle simply by changing where you stand in relation to the line you're using.

Besides tuning up your eye for flight lines, this is also excellent practice in developing a concise, consistent gun mount, which is the key to consistent shooting. The trick is to lift the gun to your cheek; don't worry about your shoulder, don't move your head, and don't look at the gun. Your cheek is the critical point of contact because that's what makes the gun point where you look, and if you can learn to cheek the stock consistently, time after time, you will just as consistently shoot where your eyes are looking.

To make this exercise optimally effective, always imagine you're going after a crossing or quartering bird. The more accustomed you are to swinging the gun instead of poking with it, the better shot you'll be. And make it a complete exercise by dry-firing with snap caps. It'll help you get reacquainted with the feel of your gun's trigger, but most important, it's good practice for making the swing-mount-fire sequence a single motion, and that's what it should be.

Spend ten or fifteen minutes every day doing this, and you'll be surprised at how smooth and fluid and ultimately deadly your gun-handling will become. You can keep it that way by doing the same thing a couple of times a week during the hunting season.

For the actual pre-season shooting, the quality of your practice is as important as the quantity. Shooting a case or more of shells is a substantial investment in both time and money, so to make it count for as much as possible, pay attention to what targets you shoot, not just how many.

Don't, for instance, go to a trap or skeet field and follow the conventions of those games by mounting your gun before you call for the targets. It's worthless as an exercise in gun-handling. You don't traipse through the woods and fields with your gun at your shoulder, nor mount it before you kick up whatever your dog's pointing. Game shooting is swing, mount and fire, and that's what you should work on.

It's also a good idea to seek out the kind of shots you get most often with the birds you hunt most often. Trap targets from the 16-yard line can be good practice for quail and prairie grouse and late-season pheasants, and skeet can be good for just about all the upland birds—but in any case, start with your gun down and ready, as if you were walking in on a point or following a flushing dog. You won't hit every target, but then you don't hit every bird, either, so forget about keeping score and concentrate on how you handle your gun.

A low-gun start is required in sporting clays, which is good, but if you're doing your training on a clays course, you'll do well to pick and choose among the various target presentations it has to offer. Look for the ones that are most like the birds you'll be hunting, and concentrate on them. Incoming and crossing tower shots are great for dove shooters and wildfowlers, all but useless to a quail hunter. Rising targets, like springing teal, are good for woodcock, but not for doves. Quartering, going-away, or crossing shots that present a target anywhere from fifteen to about thirty-five yards are dandy for quail, pheasant, and grouse.

Trap or skeet often are less expensive than sporting clays, and in some areas are more accessible, but to get the maximum benefit from trap or skeet, you'll need to get creative. And that's best done when you and one or two like-minded chums can have a field all to yourself.

Trap offers the most limited options, simply because all the targets are going-away risers, but if you can safely stand off to one side of the trap house, some of the quartering targets will become crossers. It's good practice for quail, and you can make the shots even more quail-like by standing right behind or next to the trap house. If pheasants and prairie grouse are your game, use these same angles but back off about ten yards.

Years ago, one of my hunting partners and I came up with what turned out to be an excellent way to use a skeet field in getting tuned up for grouse and woodcock, or actually for any bird you hunt while walking.

The shooter starts at one of the shooting stations and walks toward Station 8, in the center of the field. The puller can release targets at any time before the shooter gets to the middle, and it's puller's choice whether they come from the high house, low house, or both.

The shooter reloads when he gets to the center, starts walking back the way he came, and takes two more targets, once again puller's choice of which and when, before he arrives back where he started.

The puller's job, of course, is to catch the shooter at the most awkward moment, in mid-step or with his weight on the wrong foot, just as birds often do when we're hunting. The shooter can use the sound of the trap just as hunters key in on the whir of flushing wings, but then he has to locate it, read the flight line, get his feet and body properly oriented, swing and mount and fire, all before the target reaches the boundary stake.

It's not easy shooting, but it's birdlike shooting, and that's the point. One of the greatest benefits apart from just getting familiar with your gun is that you'll soon learn you have more time than you think, and I daresay most of the shots we fluff at game birds happen because we feel rushed and flustered and therefore make some fundamental error in technique. The cooler your head when a bird's in the air, the more likely you are to kill it neatly.

A word of caution: Be especially sure to wear shooting glasses if you try this little game. It's easy to get showered with shards of broken targets, and those little bits of pitch and graphite are sharp as glass.

If you want to get really creative, you and your hunting pals can have a great time with a portable trap, preferably one you can trip with a long cord. It's the best of all ways to tailor exactly the shots you need.

For instance, quail and pheasant hunters can set up a trap in a tallgrass meadow and take turns walking in, as if to a pointing dog, while the other springs the targets with a trip-cord. For best practice, the shooter should then load the trap, and become the puller, so the next guy doesn't know how many targets he'll see or which direction they'll go.

Targets launched from a hill, a bluff, or even a rooftop can be remarkably dove- and duck-like. Just remember that a manual trap means somebody's out there with it, and if you're working on incomers, make sure you don't shoot toward the trapper.

Woodcock hunters can do their thing by setting the trap to throw as nearly vertical as possible and placing it in a grove of trees, the thicker the better, and taking turns walking in. For grouse, just lower the angle and stay in the trees. If you hunt ruffs in the kind of woolly stuff I do, trying to get on the target before it smashes against a tree trunk or branch is an excellent exercise in focus, concentration, and the ability to get your gun into action with minimal delay.

I'm one of those hard-core types who starts showing withdrawal symptoms if I go ten days without pulling a trigger or sniffing nitro-powder smoke, and therefore shoot skeet and sporting clays all summer long, but around mid-August I forsake the games for their own sake and start shooting bird-targets exclusively. If I don't, my opening-day shooting will not be up to the level of skill that game birds demand, nor the level of respect they deserve.

And that would be a pity, because opening days are few enough in a lifetime, and birds too precious. Getting ready for the seasons in your head is the easy part; getting ready with your gun takes some work, but it's the only way to make those lovely autumn days all they were meant to be.

28

Sport Most Elegant

If there's anything dull about driven shooting, I haven't yet discovered what it might be. And possibly because I get to do it only a few times every year, I'm inclined to savor every moment, including the utterly delicious feeling of anticipation I get just from dressing for the day. I love the little ritual of pulling on thick, knitted, knee-high socks and tying the garters in a way that leaves the fringed ends hanging just so; of donning breeks and a crisp white shirt with traditional Tattersall check; of knotting a necktie or a bandanna around my throat; shrugging into a lightweight sweater and pulling on my old green rubber Wellies. Then I will admire myself shamelessly in the mirror for a moment and head down the stairs of some estate house or inn toward the smell of coffee and breakfast, feeling like a man who has hold of the world in exactly the right place.

Driven shooting is now more accessible, and more afford-able, than ever before—not only in such traditional venues as England, Scotland, Ireland, and parts of western Europe but, now that the Soviet Union is only a bad memory, in eastern Europe as well. This, to my mind, is one of the best things that's happened to the gunning world in a long time.

To Americans, nurtured as we are in a sporting tradition that has never included anything more formal than Southern quail hunting, driven shooting seems exotic and perhaps a bit intimidating. Exotic it is, in some purely wonderful ways, and intimidating it can be, at least the first time and especially if you don't really know what to expect.

Perhaps because it was for so long available only to the ultra-rich, the general view of driven shooting saw it with some taint of snobbery. I remember reading some pretty silly maga-zine stories in the 1960s and '70s that essentially made fun of its traditions, or implied that it's little more than wholesale slaughter, or that our egalitarian principles should be offended by the very idea of beaters and loaders and others providing sport for only a handful of guns.

Fortunately, this kind of nonsense has all but faded away, as more and more of us have discovered that the traditions derive from a deeply-felt love of hunting and shooting and from a profound respect for the game; that well-presented driven birds offer some of the most demanding shooting there is; that, far from representing any sort of class oppression, serving as a beater or loader is an important source of income, either for the individuals or for their hunting clubs.

What you shoot also depends upon where you go. Scotland and northern England have a lock on driven grouse. Spain is the classic venue for red-legged partridge, though you'll find them on some English estates as well. Denmark arguably has the finest driven duck shooting in the world, and no country offers woodcock shooting to match what you'll find in southern England.

To an extent, these are specialty birds, in specialized locations. For the most widely available shooting, the pheasant is unquestionably king. Unlike the others, pheasants can be hatched, released, and reared to assure continually high populations. These are not the hapless patsies too often found on American game farms. Though they're regularly fed, these birds customarily live on their own, in the wild, from the time they're about two months old, and by shooting season there is no discernable difference between them and purely wild birds when it comes to power on the wing. It's the same everywhere.

The objective is the same everywhere, too—send the birds over the guns flying as fast as they can and as high as possible. The more they look, from the shooter's point of view, like long-tailed flies, the better. The tallest pheasants I've seen were in the hillier parts of England—in Devon and Somerset and Cornwall, for instance, where estates have been managed for shooting for a hundred years or more. There, the valley floors and slopes are sown in grass to be cropped by grazing sheep while the hilltops are left wooded above an understory dense with brush. In these hanging coverts, as they're called, the birds are tended, fed, protected from predators, and otherwise husbanded. They soon learn that their escape route is a flight from one hilltop to another, and few of them dawdle on the way. It may be as much as sixty yards down to where the guns are stationed along the bottom of the valleys.

In other, less vertical parts of the world, a clever game-keeper can present pheasants at perfectly respectable elevations by taking advantage of tall trees and other features of the landscape. I've seen this done especially well on the Tisza Plain of Hungary, which for the most part is flat as last month's beer. Being open-country birds, pheasants invariably will fly over a stand of timber rather than through the treetops, and Hungarian shooting clubs manage their grounds and shoots accordingly. The holding covers, to which the birds naturally gravitate for safety, are placed well out from the woodlots to give them plenty of distance for climbing after they're flushed. The guns, in turn, are positioned right at the edge of the woods, where the shots can only come as the birds are reaching maximum height.

On the reverse side of the same situation, the guns may be stationed on the far side of the woods, so the birds don't come into view until they're nearly overhead and smoking along at top speed. If there's a sizable stand of relatively short trees, the keepers may place the guns along a narrow alley cut through the middle. Thanks to dense woods, you don't see the birds until they're right on top of you, and since it doesn't take a pheasant long to cover fifty feet or so, they're often gone before you can react. Under those circumstances, a twenty-yard bird can be as sporty as one flying twice as high.

In any case, they need no encouragement to fly fast, and if you harbor any notion that driven birds may be too easy, it won't take many blazing overhead at seventy miles per hour to change your mind.

The daily bag can range from about three hundred birds to a thousand or more, depending upon how much you choose to spend. Sheer numbers, though, are one thing, while excellent quality is something else. If high birds are one benchmark, the pace at which they're presented is yet another. Seeing several hundred pheasants blow out of a single covert all at once is a stirring sight, but it doesn't offer the best shooting. Ideally, the birds should come up a few at a time from the beginning of a drive until the end. Achieving that is a form of art.

Pheasants being what they are, they don't want to flush in a steady cadence. They much prefer to run until they reach the edge of their cover and then fly, so the first few minutes of a drive are almost always birdless. Even with the deftest handling, they tend to stack up at the end, so the trick is to push them just enough to prompt steady flushes yet not bear down so hard that they all blast off at the same time. It's not easy. A good team of experienced beaters work together with the precision and delicacy of a ballet troupe, and they're worth their weight in any precious substance you can name.

Not surprisingly, a fair set of traditions have accrued over the past 150 years, and every one of them contributes in some way to achieving the best and safest level of sport. Even traditional modes of dress are designed to keep a shooter optimally

warm, dry, and able to handle his gun readily. I always recommend that first-timers get up a proper outfit before they go.
No one will make you feel out of place if you don't, but it's all
part of the experience, and there's no reason not to go for the
whole thing, starting from the ground up.

That can mean brogues or low-top leather boots when
the weather is dry, but for the most part you'll be in a chilly
climate at a season that can be rainy, even snowy at times, and
therefore frequently muddy underfoot, so it's always wise to
have a pair of Wellington boots—knee-high, rubber, well-
fitting in the foot and snug in the pipes. You won't do a lot of
walking, but you will do some, so good fit is important.

In part, this means a close fit at the ankle and calf, which
is why good Wellies have narrow pipes. And because stuffing
trouser bottoms into narrow boots is a losing battle and uncomfortable besides, you'll want to wear breeks instead of long
pants. Breeks are simply truncated trousers that fasten snugly
just below the knee, and you wear them with heavy, over-the-
knee stockings. If the breeks are cut to a fairly loose fit, you'll
never put on anything more comfortable. They're great for
walking. I often wear them hunting quail and pheasants on wet
or snowy days.

(One bit of advice: If you shoot in England, it's best not to
refer to breeks as "knickers." That's what we call them, short
for "knickerbockers," but in the British idiom "knickers"
are the feminine undergarments we call "panties." You can
imagine the spin this might put on a conversation with your
fellow guns.)

Beyond the breeks, you can either go whole-hog and buy a
Norfolk-style tweed shooting jacket to match, or simply wear
a sweater. Either way, you can top it off with a waxed-cotton
coat and stay warm, dry, and well dressed in even the foulest
weather. I prefer the sweater and cotton coat, myself.

In Britain, everyone shoots wearing a necktie; on the
Continent, some do and some don't. I wear one in England,
because that's the custom, but otherwise I much prefer just

tying a bandanna around my neck. It's warmer and a lot more comfortable besides.

I don't like wearing a hat when I shoot, but it's always a good idea to have one in case of rain, either a wool motoring cap or one of waxed cotton with a full brim.

Leather shooting gloves are useful, especially if you shoot a side-by-side gun; on some drives, your barrels will get too hot to hold bare-handed. Earplugs are a good idea as well, and shooting glasses are a must. A lot of shoots require that guns be cased between drives, so you should take along a padded gunslip.

In some places—Britain, for instance—only break-action guns are permitted; that's for safety, not snobbishness. It doesn't matter whether it's a side-by-side or over/under, just so long as it's a break-open gun. In eastern Europe, where the shooting is a bit less formal, repeating guns are not banned, but they aren't greatly appreciated, either. Again, it's solely for reasons of safety.

As the first order of business, you'll be assigned a loader. He carries all the cartridges, and your gun whenever you're not shooting. If the bags are high enough to warrant using two guns, your loader will show you the standard drill for passing them back and forth safely and efficiently. Essentially, you give him a gun with your right hand (assuming you're right-handed) and take the other from him with your left.

If you're only using one, the loader will stand just behind you and a bit to the side, with fresh cartridges ready. (In England, a one-gun loader is typically called a "stuffer.") You take your shots, open the gun, eject the empties, and turn slightly, holding the gun so he can drop new rounds in. It takes a bit of practice, but once you get the hang of how to do it with minimal motion, you'll be surprised at how quickly you're back in action. The trick is to keep your eyes on the birds and let the loader do his job.

The other trick is to develop the habit of closing your gun by lifting the butt rather than the barrels. That way, the muzzles are pointing safely at the ground in case it goes off as you close it—and a sticky firing pin or a worn sear can make that happen.

Your loader also will show you your stand for each drive,

point out where the birds will come from, advise on which ones are rightfully yours and which are better left to neighboring guns, and in general do everything he can to see that you have a good time and a successful shoot.

It's very important that you don't move off your peg unless the loader tells you it's okay. With other guns nearby and a lot of people out in front, being where you shouldn't be can lead to an accident.

At the better British shoots, and at some on the Continent, the pickers-up will stand by on each drive with retrievers waiting primly at heel. Neither will move until the drive is over, but the picker-up will know exactly where all your birds are. On the Continent, at least in all the shooting I've done there, the pickers-up seldom use dogs. Instead, they simply keep track of downed birds and do the retrieving themselves.

The rules of safety are absolute. You do not load your gun until you hear the horn signal the beginning of a drive, and when the same horn signals the end, you stop shooting and unload, even if there are a few birds still coming out. The general rule is that you shoot no lower than about forty-five degrees, nor fire unless you can see plenty of sky below the bird, nor, if there are trees in front, shoot at any angle less than treetop height. The steeper the land, the higher your shots need to be. On some drives, it's safe to turn around and take going-away shots; ask your loader and if it is okay, remember to point your barrels straight up as you turn.

Although the loaders and beaters and pickers-up are usually experienced, you still need to be on guard. Having flocks of birds streaming overhead is incredibly exciting, and nobody is immune. Once, in Hungary, the young woman who was my picker-up got so revved up by the shooting that she was almost dancing with excitement, and I was enjoying her enthusiasm until she went to get a bird that fell a few feet in front of the line of guns, while other birds were still in the air. I was willing to overlook the breach of safety and simply keep an eye out for her, just because she was obviously having such a good time, but the shoot-master was not. Whatever dressing-down she got was in private (and in Magyar), but during the next drive she was as demure and circumspect as a novitiate. It's not in my nature to rain on anyone's picnic, but the shoot-master was right; nobody should break the rules of safety.

Bottom line is that you must always, always, keep your wits about you, because getting rattled into taking a bad shot is easier than you think. Low birds are not considered sporting in the first place, but they can tempt you sorely. I once saw a man lose his head on a low bird crossing to his right and bag two Italians and a guy from Florida with a single shot. Fortunately, no one was seriously hurt, but the injuries weren't mere nicks, either. It could as easily have cost someone an eye or a life, and that's definitely not in the interest of good sport.

Your loader will be watching you closely, and though he'll be polite about it, he won't hesitate to admonish you for even a marginally unsafe shot. That's as it should be. Don't get offended if he warns you but don't forget it, either. Persist, and he will refuse you any more cartridges. I've seen that happen, too, and it was an enormous relief to everybody.

There have been lots of funny stories written by one-timers about the formalities of driven shooting—funny but unfortunate, because they've created in this country a notion that it's all stuffy formality in which the tiniest lapse of etiquette is met with reprisal at a Carthaginian level. Nonsense. There is certainly a code of behavior that's expected, but it involves little more than being safe and fundamentally polite so that everyone has an opportunity for good, safe shooting.

Placement naturally varies a bit according to the terrain, but you always have at least one neighboring gun, usually two, and you'll typically be twenty to forty yards apart. Your field of fire is the zone straight in front of you, fanning out halfway to your neighbors on either side. Birds in that zone are yours; those outside it are someone else's opportunities, and poaching is highly impolite. There are always toss-ups, of course, but deliberately shooting birds clearly out of your zone is bad manners, poor sportsmanship.

Poaching can also be a matter of thoughtlessness, which is

perhaps more forgivable but no less annoying. On one drive a few years ago, I was second gun in the line, and the first gun, on my right, was a man I'd shot with before and knew to be rather inconsiderate of his neighbors—not necessarily on purpose, just sufficiently wound up in himself to be thoughtless.

Rather than coming straight on, most of the birds at our end came at just enough angle that most of mine flew through his zone first. The polite thing to do was let at least half of those on the left pass, particularly as he had everything on his right to himself, but he shot at every one, regardless of which side it was on.

I don't normally make much issue of rudeness, but after about twenty pheasants flared or died just as I was beginning to swing on them, I got a bit irritated and, using my choked left barrel, started poaching birds in his zone, taking them far out, just as he was beginning to swing. The first time or two, I could see his shoulders twitch in surprise, and after a couple more, he finally turned and looked at me. I shook my finger at him, and could see his face change as he realized what he'd been doing.

After that, he left most, though not all, of the left-side birds alone and even offered a grudging sort of semi-apology when the drive was over. (I shot with him again a couple of years later and, on a drive when we were again neighboring guns, took a quietly fiendish pleasure in watching him miss every bird that flew past.) The moral to that story: Know where your neighbors are and be considerate of them.

Actually, the formalities are at least half the fun, especially the rituals performed in honor of the game. In eastern Europe and in some parts of the western Continent as well, every shoot ends with a tableau. The day's birds are laid out neatly, respectfully, in a graceful arrangement, and everyone involved pays tribute to them with speeches, toasts, and traditional music. It's an honest expression of what we all feel, and a beautiful thing to take part in.

So, the shooting is only one element—the central one, but still only a part. The others are just as important to the overall experience.

An old friend of mine summed it up several years ago in Hungary, on his first driven shoot. We had a rainy day, which is never the ideal, but it's part of the game. We came in at lunchtime to a tiny clubhouse about as inelegant as the headquarters of a Louisiana duck club. But there was a big iron pot of aromatic wild-boar stew simmering over an open fire outdoors and copious jugs of fresh, raw, wonderful red wine waiting indoors.

We were all wet, chilled and justifiably miserable, but the morning's drives had produced pheasants brave and beautiful, and we all felt the glow that only such shooting can produce. I was standing next to a little wood stove, warming the outside with its scant heat and the inside with wine, when Bob moved in next to me, his own glass of wine in hand.

He looked like a drowned cat, wringing wet, dripping rainwater from every place where water could drip, wearing a beatific smile that could make Buddha envious.

He took a slurp of wine, held his hands to the stove, and shivered. I said it was a pity he had to have his first driven shoot on such an awful day. He looked at me, still smiling.

And my friend Bob said, "This is better than sex."

Well, I'm not sure about that, but it's better than almost anything else you can do standing up. For me, the moments are in the anticipation and the afterglow. As I said at the start, I love the process of dressing for a shoot. I really do. But even sweeter are the moments after, when you straggle back to the lodge or estate house or hotel deliciously tired, hungry, often cold, sometimes wet. Then, you pour yourself something neat and strong and find if you can an open fire to watch while you sip your drink.

By that point, my sense of anticipation is focused on the prospects of a hot shower and a good dinner, but I seldom feel in any rush to get them. These plangent moments at the end, like those at the beginning, are moments on the cusp between days rare and beautiful, days that come too seldom and pass too quickly.

29

AMERICAN ZZ

Of all the games played with a shotgun, none are more challenging nor more exciting than those in which the target is a live pigeon. Of these, columbaire, hand-thrown birds, is arguably the more difficult, because it involves the additional element of professional throwers with pitching arms that any Major Leaguer would be happy to own. For my part, I find box birds challenging enough.

The layouts vary a bit from place to place, but the game essentially comprises five to nine traps, each capable of holding a single pigeon, laid out in the center of a ring surrounded by a two-foot fence, which may be as close as seventeen to twenty yards from the end traps. You take your shooting position—somewhere from twenty-six to thirty-two yards back from the center trap, depending on your handicap, load and mount your gun, and call for a bird. Thereupon, the trapper springs whichever trap he's chosen at random; you never know which it'll be. When the bird takes off, you have two shots to drop it dead, or at least retrievable, inside the ring. If it crosses the fence—alive, dead, wounded, or whatever—it's counted lost. It's lost even if it manages to flutter over as the bird-boys attempt to pick it up.

Pigeons are tough, unpredictable, powerful on the wing, and capable of extraordinary aerobatics. You never know what they're going to do once they leave the trap, but whatever it is, they can do it with remarkable determination and astonishing speed. Even stone dead in the air, their momentum is often enough to carry them over the fence.

Far as I'm concerned, shooting box birds ranks among the top three most exciting things you can do while dressed and standing up, maybe even the top two.

Although proscribed in a few states, pigeon shooting is perfectly legal in many others, but the shoots are almost invariably kept low-key and semi-private to avoid attention from the animal-rights loonies whose hearts bleed at the thought of shooting a poor, innocent pigeon, and from the equally ignorant, equally self-righteous mass media. Just finding a flyer shoot can be a chore, and if you do, you'll also find it a fairly expensive pastime, what with entry fees and options. Even if you choose only to shoot practice birds for fun, you'll still end up paying five bucks or better apiece for them. The cost is why I don't shoot nearly as many box birds as I'd like, and it's one more bit of evidence in support of my theory that I was supposed to have been born rich but somebody screwed up.

The now-ubiquitous clay target was invented specifically as a substitute for live birds in the game of trap. Lots of good things have happened to it in the hundred years since, but even though a clay can be presented in some semblance of birdlike flight, its inherent limitations will forever prevent it from being truly pigeonlike. Clays start slowing down the moment they're launched; pigeons speed up. In battue form, clays can be made to turn while still rising, but they simply can't be made to fly as erratically or as eccentrically as a pigeon. More's the pity, and

to hell with a five-cent cigar: What the shooting world really needs is some kind of target capable of behaving like a pigeon.

And at last we have one. It's called ZZ; it originated in Europe, where it's known as "zed-zed"; and its most highly refined form, known as American ZZ, is a tribute to Yankee ingenuity.

A European ZZ is a target with wings. Launched from a special thrower, it spins off twisting and turning, altogether more pigeonlike than any target that came before. The whole thing is frangible, shattering when hit into a shower of pieces that resemble feathers knocked from a well-shot bird. It's cool and great fun, but difficult to find in the U.S. and almost as expensive to shoot as the real thing.

An American ZZ is also a target with wings, but it's reusable. It comprises a metal propeller, with blades pitched like an airplane prop, and a thin PVC dome, typically called a "witness" that snaps onto the propeller. The launcher looks and functions like an old-fashioned oscillating fan. With a target clipped onto the rotor, it spins at a standard rate of 5,500 rpm, which you can kick up to a maximum 6,500 rpm. The pull is controlled by a hard-wire remote, just like a standard electric clay trap. When the trapper pushes the button, the motor instantly reverses and the target goes tearing off wherever the oscillating head happens to be pointing at that moment. It can climb, dip, curve, hug the grass, pop up like a woodcock or teal, and altogether cut more didoes, chandelles, twists and turns than I've ever seen from any object not wearing feathers.

Hit it with about the same force required to break a clay target—that is, three or four shot pellets or more—and the witness breaks away from the propeller to fall more or less straight down. Really center one and the two parts not only separate but the propeller itself heels over and drops as if struck by lightning. Fringe it and you can literally hear the pellets rattle off the steel wings while the whole thing sails off to lost-land.

It's great fun, by turns immensely satisfying or beastly frustrating, altogether the most challenging inanimate target I know, and thoroughly addictive. In other words, it's just like box pigeons.

A full American ZZ layout—ten machines, a nine-machine computerized control box, wires and cables, along with 250 propellers and 500 witnesses—costs just under $15,000, which put immediate brakes on my momentary fantasy of installing one in my front pasture (and prompted me to remember the theory I mentioned earlier), but the economics are such to make it both a crowd-pleaser and a paying proposition for a gun club. The launchers are as simple and as breakdown-proof as the parlor fans they resemble. The propellers can withstand as many as ten direct hits before they no longer fly properly, and even the witnesses are reusable through as many as four or five smacks sufficient to render them dead. Installed by an active club and sold to members at $10 or $12 a round, it's an investment that could be amortized and turned to the profit column in no time. And believe me, if you've ever been bitten by the box-bird bug—or even if you haven't—you'll think a $12 round of ZZs is the bargain of the century.

A box-bird layout is only one possibility in how you con-figure the range. The standard control box comes programmed for five different games, including one that releases all the tar-gets simultaneously. By comparison, a quail-flush setup using clay targets will put you to sleep; an American ZZ flush is as wonderful a piece of chaos as you can find this side of wild bobwhites.

You can buy the launchers in smaller numbers, and the only limits are those of your own creativity. It would require a goodly amount of cable to wire everything together, but I can imagine a quail, grouse, or woodcock walk to end them all, using ZZ launchers placed strategically in an acre of brush or mixed brush and sapling trees. Unlike even sporting clays, which can grow humdrum if the presentations or shooting stands aren't changed periodically, I suspect you could set up a ZZ walk, with re-leases entirely trapper's choice, that you could shoot for the rest of your life and never be able to fully anticipate.

Because it's a new game requiring new equipment, finding an American ZZ layout may be even more difficult right now than finding a flyer shoot. To locate one, or to find your nearest dealer, contact the manufacturer: American ZZ Corp., 171 Spring Hill Road, Trumbull, Connecticut 06611, phone 203-261-1058, fax 203-452-9359.

And you can tell 'em I sent you, which will at least be good for a chuckle as they describe having witnessed the fastest and possibly severest case of target addiction ever acquired in North America. I was a goner for box birds years ago and really didn't need yet one more shooting game to haunt my dreams. But if it had to be, I can't think of any better than this.

30

Being Shot

Being shot is a curious feeling. I don't mean sprinkled with spent pellets, as often happens in a dove field and as sometimes happens in a duck marsh—I mean being in the path of a shot swarm traveling roughly parallel to the ground and being struck by pellets very much unspent. It feels like getting whacked by a hammer. It makes you think about things.

It certainly reminds you that hunting involves an element of danger. In hunting there are no firing lines, and guns are almost always loaded. Except for dove, turkey, and driven shooting, upland hunting involves almost continual movement in environments where companions lose sight of one another, sometimes momentarily, sometimes longer. Upland birds flush from the ground and frequently present shots at about the same height as the upper body of a standing man.

As hunters, we accept all this as the reality of our sport, and as good hunters we take it as our primary responsibility not to endanger our fellow hunters or dogs.

Which is more complex than it might sound. It begins with accepting the facts that firearms are inherently dangerous items and that there is no substitute, mechanical or otherwise, for safe gun-handling. And safe gun-handling, like Professor Harold Hill's iron-clad leave from a three-rail billiard shot, takes judgement, brains, and maturity. Judgement always looks beyond the target, imagining who or what may be in the line of fire. Brains knows exactly how the gun works, knows that you can slam-fire a Model 12 Winchester, that an autoloader with a worn sear can go full-auto in a blink, or that any break-action with a sticky striker can go off when you close it. Brains never goes afield with a gun known to be mechanically faulty. Maturity owns restraint and an unfailing belief that no game bird in the bag is worth even a fraction of risk.

Safe gun-handling is a responsibility that cannot be abrogated. All the puling of the whiners and the machinations of their lawyers aside, a shooting accident is never the fault of the people who built the gun or those who made the cartridges. To argue thus is worthy of no respect, and the fact that any court would accept it as valid is a disgraceful state of affairs. A poorly designed automobile that goes out of control without warning is one thing; a gun that goes off when it's not supposed to is another. When a car takes over, the driver can only go where it does, like it or not, but a gun can't point itself. With the muzzle pointed in a safe direction, every shot is a safe one, whether it's deliberate or accidental.

But still it's not quite even that simple, for even though the responsibility can't be abrogated, it certainly can be shared—which is why we wear highly visible colors, don't wander around as if we're browsing a shopping mall, keep track of our partners, continually communicate our whereabouts, and otherwise take pains to keep ourselves out of harm's way.

But then there's sheer happenstance, conjunctions of circumstances no one could predict. Such events usually are explainable after the fact, but that's not necessarily much comfort, and the explanations aren't always entirely satisfying. Being by nature a fatalist, a view I believe I inherited from the Irish branch of my family tree, I'm perfectly comfortable with the notion that whatever happens was somehow meant to happen, but even after all these years, I still don't have a clue why fate ordained that I should be shot by one of the best hunters I've ever known or why such a careful, serious man should have been the one to pull the trigger.

We were three old friends, partners of many years' standing, hunting grouse in a long, narrow strip of woods between two pastures. I've known the place almost as long as I've known the partners, but only in the past few years has it come of an age to harbor birds. Before, it was a patch of scrub we walked in order to get from one covert to another. It was always worth a look in the really flush years; when there were young birds everywhere, at least one was naive enough to think he could spend a winter in that thin, chilly place. Now, though, it's a real covert, and we came to it that afternoon knowing full well that some birds were waiting out ahead. One hunter took the far pasture edge, another the center, and I the near edge. The man who has the toughest going sets the pace, so we strolled along the outside, keeping track of his progress—and therefore our relative positions—by the sound of crackling brush.

As I sometimes do when I'm tired, I got fixated on my feet, on how the blunt toes of my old, scuffed-up Bean boots looked pushing through the popple leaves scattered in the grass, lulled into a reverie of dog bells and warm sunshine and a peaceful feeling. I came out of it to the sound of a shot off to the right, instinctively turned that way to see what there was to see, and felt something slam against my face and chest.

It did not, strictly speaking, knock me off my feet, but I went down nonetheless. I knew without thinking that I'd been shot and felt a momentary wonder at the absence of pain.

It was frightening, but that proved momentary, too. Pushing up to my hands and knees, I watched blood drip and spatter onto the leaves, fascinated at how bright it looked, red on yellow, scarlet on gold. I put my hand to my cheek and stared at the smear of blood that came away on my glove, impossibly bright against the sweat-stained leather. More drips onto the leaves, steady, hypnotic. I could hear them pattering, which in my strange state of detachment seemed remarkable.

Probably no more than half a minute passed before my head began to clear, but I don't really know. Time simply stopped for a while, then started again. I stripped off my gloves, dug my bandanna out of my hip pocket, and pressed it hard to my cheek. By the time my friends stepped out of the woods to find me sitting there in the grass, all the fogginess was gone, replaced by an equally odd feeling of serenity.

"What's the matter?" one asked.

"Who shot?"

"I did," the other said.

"It hit me."

I don't believe I've ever seen a face take on a more stricken look. First came a wave of utter astonishment and disbelief, replaced by the sort of pain that only comes from deep inside. He looked at the bloody leaves, then back at me, knelt down, eyes brimming, and said very slowly, "My dear friend, I am so sorry."

I've known this man for a long, long time. He is practically the definition of a keen hunter, a good hunter, a safe hunter, to say nothing of being a fine and treasured friend. He will carry a thorn from that moment for the rest of his life, and the thought of it nearly broke my heart.

We all sat there for a while, lit our pipes like some council of elders musing on the ineffable turns of fate, and put the pieces together to form a picture. The explanation was both prosaic and fantastic.

We were fifty yards apart, both walking in the open but separated by brush and woods so dense that neither of us could see the faintest speck of the other's blaze-orange vest. The bird flushed nearly at his feet, quartering ahead, offering an angle and elevation that anyone would take to be a perfectly safe shot.

Except it wasn't, and by then I knew exactly why. Because I let my attention wander, I had gradually got farther ahead of the man in the middle than I realized and certainly farther ahead than the man on the far side had any reason to believe I'd be. It was my job to stay out of his field of fire, and I didn't do it.

So much for the prosaic. The fantastic grows ever more bemusing the more we think and talk about it, a set of circumstances that might never come together again in exactly the same way if we lived another hundred years and hunted every day of our lives. And if even one circumstance had been the merest bit different, the whole thing would never have happened.

There is, of course, the matter of the bird being just where it was and flying just where it did, but the fact that shots at game birds come at entirely random angles is just one reason why it's called "hunting" and not "skeet shooting." The fantastic things are truly fantastic.

One is the gun he was carrying. It wasn't his; it was mine. It was new at the time. I'd carried it for a couple of days, found it highly effective for grouse, and because the same stock prescription fits us both, I offered it to my pal that day thinking he'd enjoy it, too. It's a 12-bore of 6½ pounds that handles with an almost perfect balance of speed and smoothness. He fired it three times and killed three grouse; the third shot was the one that hit me.

But as he said later, "If I'd been carrying my old Parker, I'd never even have fired. The cover's so dense that I couldn't have got it moving and ahead of the bird before it was out of sight."

Maybe I have a more highly tuned sense of irony than most, or maybe I've just absorbed a few hundred too many jolts of recoil, but the notion that I got myself shot with my own gun because of its wonderful handling qualities strikes me as purely delicious, a quirk that O. Henry, Alfred Hitchcock, and Kurt Vonnegut all together would be hard-pressed to match.

It's equally fantastic that I managed to get ahead of my companions. You wouldn't know this unless you'd actually hunted with me, but anyone who has would tell you I'm an inveterate ambler, as pottery as a twenty-year-old dog. I've never hunted with someone confined to a wheelchair, but if I did, he'd never have to ask me to slow down. It's a sign of my friends' good grace that they put up with me, I'm so poky. But that one time...

It's fantastic, too, that any pellets got through at all. The bird stopped some, the trees and brush most of the rest. Had they been No. 8s instead of 7½, or soft lead instead of hard copper-clads, maybe none would have made the whole distance. But at least three somehow managed to traverse that ungodly tangle without hitting anything until they got to me. One struck just below my right cheekbone about an inch below the lens of my shooting glasses. That one produced all the blood, as head wounds do. Another missed the vee of my vest-front by a mere fraction, went through a canvas shirt and a T-shirt to lodge just left of my sternum. The third nicked the heel of my right hand; had I not been holding my gun in that hand with the barrels resting on my shoulder, it would have missed me altogether.

Had I been where I was supposed to be or if any other single circumstance were different, they all would have missed me, and one old friend would have been spared the anguish of shooting another. I don't know if I've convinced him that I have more to apologize for than he does, but I know he won't forget it. Neither will I.

We will live with it and go on being hunters and friends and go on trying to figure out what we're supposed to learn from it. So far, the best either of us can do is fall back on an old cliché, which, like most clichés, happens to be true: Sometimes, things just happen.

31

USEFUL
HABITS

Prevailing opinion in some quarters has it that if there were no bad habits, I would have no habits at all. This is not true, or at least not entirely. I have some habits that are good by almost any definition. My mother, for instance, instilled in me a firm commitment to at least one shower every day and an invariable habit of lifting the seat, flushing, and closing the lid. Dad taught me to be always aware of where I'm pointing a gun. My wife has trained me to use sunscreen religiously. My dog has made me thoroughly Pavlovian about the fact that five o'clock is dinnertime (hers).

The list goes on, and it even includes some habits I've developed all on my own, without adult supervision. Perhaps not surprisingly, several of them have to do with guns and shooting, which means there is a point to this roundabout approach (a habit most of my editors consider to be less than desirable, but I'd rather not go into that right now). Some of these are aimed at self-preservation, others at achieving the most from my meager skills, and they seem to me useful enough to share.

I don't know when it started, but I have become an utter fussbudget about looking down my gunbarrels. I do it every time I pull a gun out of a case, every time I drop in a fresh cartridge, every time I reload after I've propped a gun against a tree or laid it in the grass. I've even acquired the habit of opening my gun every so often while hunting, shaking out the shells and peering down the bores. I didn't realize this until one of my companions mentioned it last season.

"That's the third time you've done that in the past hour," he said. "What the hell are you looking for?"

Nothing, actually, or at least nothing is what I hope to see. I'm looking for sweet daylight down the bores, unobstructed by twigs, grass, chaff, snow, even a wisp of fluff from a gun case lining, or a stray scrap from the last cartridge I fired.

Stuff happens, as I was reminded a month after my friend pointed out my compulsive peeking. We were shooting driven birds in Europe. One of the guns, a thoroughly experienced shot whom I've known for some time, was using a lovely old Boss that I'd give my eyeteeth to own, and shooting with his customary skill. But in the midst of a drive, he corked off a dud. As his stand was far from mine at the time, I can only assume that neither he nor his loader noticed the squib in the steady thump from neighboring guns and the thrilling stream of pheasants rocketing high overhead. At any rate, the loader dropped in a pair of fresh rounds, and his next shot opened a sickening gash in the right barrel.

Fortunately, the barrels were still stout enough that the thinnest section of wall was well ahead of his leading hand, and he was using a handguard besides, so the only casualty was the gun and, considering what a new pair of best-quality London barrels costs these days, most of the pleasure in his shooting trip. It was scary nonetheless.

Had he been nearer, I might have noticed his dud cartridge because I seem to have formed an unconscious habit of listening to every shot I hear. I don't know when this one got started either, but unless someone else fires at the same instant I do, I've become hypersensitive to anything that doesn't sound right, even through my earplugs. I've been known to scream "Don't shoot!" at the top of my lungs on clays courses and game fields just because some shot didn't sound quite kosher, and I've earned a fair share of odd looks either because of pointing out the obvious or because of misinterpreting perfectly normal shots. That's okay. Having the chance to spare someone an injury to himself or his gun is worth any amount of embarrassment and besides, a certain license to be eccentric is part of the reward for having earned all this gray hair.

I also have a habit of frequently running my thumb over the safety slide to be sure it's in the ON position. Unlike most others, I know exactly where that one comes from. Once upon a time, flush with the confidence and partial brainlessness of youth, I used to check my safety by pulling the trigger— confident because Dad's incessant drilling meant that my muzzles were never, ever pointed where a stray shot could do harm to companion or dog; brainless because checking your safety that way is about as bright as checking the level of a gas tank by tossing in a lighted match.

These digital investigations went off just fine till one day about thirty years ago. That time, the gun went off. It was pointed safely, but the whole thing scared the bejeezus out of me and earned a well-deserved dressing-down from my companion who, thankfully, was not Dad. If he'd been there,

I'd have been field-dressed and roasted on a spit, twenty-odd years old or not.

I've also had guns go off when I closed them, once because of a firing pin gone sticky after three days of hunting in rain and once because of a faulty sear. Those scared the bejeezus out of me, too, and always serve as a reminder that sparing stress to action joint and fastening system isn't the only good reason for closing a gun gently.

Having seen dogs and people accidentally shot, and having been shot myself, leaves me convinced there's no such thing as being too cautious with a gun. Or to put it another way and paraphrase an old joke, just because you're not paranoid doesn't mean an accident isn't out to get you. It's a form of paranoia I can live with.

If some habits help make a safer shooter, some others can help make a better shot. Actually, there are lots of those, but two in particular have been especially useful to me. I learned them from my old friend Jack Mitchell, and I've spent about ten years making them second nature, as much an unconscious part of my shooting technique as clicking off the safety while lifting the gun to my cheek.

The first is doing exactly that: lifting the gun to my cheek and keeping my head dead-still. As in any exercise of eye-hand coordination, we can point a finger or a gun most accurately when either the hand or the eye is a fixed point of reference. In order to track a moving object, the hand obviously has to move, which means the eye needs to be steady. You can see what I mean with a little exercise I use in shooting schools. Keep your head still and point your index finger at some small object in the distance, arm fully extended. Notice how accurate you are; if your finger was a gun barrel, you'd probably drill your object dead-center.

But then put your head in motion, side to side, around, up and down, and try the same thing. Notice how difficult it is to have any accuracy at all as your finger follows your eyes. That's just what happens every time you heed the old edict about bringing the stock to your shoulder and dropping your head to the comb. It's okay if you're aiming a rifle but not worth a damn if you're pointing a gun at a moving target.

Good habit: Raise the gun to your cheek; don't move your head to the gun.

Another: Let your first move toward the target be with the hand that's holding the barrels. A good gun "mount" is actually a swing and mount, all in one motion. First put your eyes on the target, and do nothing till you see the flight line. Then start your forward hand on its task—which is to move the barrels from where the target was to where it is to where it will be when the shot charge gets there.

If you make the mount and swing a two-part move—that is, slam the gun to your shoulder and then start after the bird—you're behind from the start; your likelihood of catching up, much less passing it, begins at Slim and progresses quickly to In Your Dreams.

But let your leading hand truly lead and make your trigger hand simply follow along, and you've already tracked and caught the target by the time the gun touches your cheek and shoulder. Keep up the momentum, look at the air where that bird will be in the next moment, slap the trigger, and there's an excellent chance your dog will shortly be searching for a dead bird.

At that point, you're entitled to the wingshooter's version of spiking a ball in the end zone. Rock back on your heels, lift your eyes in a smile of thanks to the red gods, thumb the top lever, and catch the empty as the ejector kicks. Unless you think there might be a late flusher in the grass, take your time about reloading and savor the moment.

But either way, give the barrel a glance before you drop another one in. It's a habit that can spare you some grief.

Part III

ODDS & ENDS

ODDS & ENDS

In general, shotguns and shooting make up an enormous subject, but the bits and pieces thereof don't always qualify as subjects for chapters all their own. It's frustrating at times to find that some of the most interesting odds and ends are just that—items too small to merit more than a page or two, but yet too intriguing in one way or another to ignore altogether. That's what this section is all about.

CHOKE DIMENSIONS

Most of us think of shotgun chokes as classes—skeet, improved-cylinder, modified, full, and so on. For those who actually make guns, this is entirely too vague; they need something specific, quantifiable, measurable. It's one thing to know that choke designations refer to the percentage of a shot charge that prints inside a thirty-inch circle at forty yards, quite another to know exactly how much muzzle constriction is required to achieve those results.

In gunmakers' terms, here are the standard dimensions as recognized and identified by some of the world's major gun trades.

WORLD STANDARDS, 12-GAUGE

PERCENTAGE	CONSTRICTION	U.S.	U.K.	FN	ITALY
40%	.000–.004	Cyl	True Cyl	★★★	CL
50%	.008–.012	I-C	I-C	★★_	★★★★
55%	.016–.020	M	1/4	★★	★★★
60%	.021–.025	M	1/2	★★	★★★
65%	.029–.033	I-M	3/4	★_	★★
70%	.037–.040	F	F	★	★
70%+	.041–	E-F	E-F		

28-GAUGE, LONDON PROOF HOUSE

(.543" minimum, .563" maximum, .550" nominal)

Cyl	.000–.002
SK1	.003–.004
I-C	.005–.006
SK2	.007–.011
M	.012–.015
I-M	.016–.021
F	.022–

WINCHESTER

CHOKE	PERCENTAGE @ 40 YARDS
Cyl	35%
I-C	43%
SK1	33%
SK2	50%

WINCHESTER

GAUGE	CHOKE	CONSTRICTION
12	I-C	.004–.006
	M	.010–.015
	I-M	.015–.018
	F	.031–.036
16	I-C	.004–.006
	M	.010–.015
	I-M	.015–.018
	F	.025–.035
20	I-C	.004–.006
	M	.007–.012
	I-M	.012–.015
	F	.020–.030

BRITISH AND AMERICAN SHOT SIZES

Describing the English and Americans as peoples of similar heritage separated by a common language is more than just a witty comment. In some instances, it's absolutely true. Most shooters know that the English designations of shot size are different from ours. The rule of thumb is that theirs refer to pellets one size smaller than ours; an English No. 6 actually is the equivalent of an American No. 7, but the comparisons aren't always so neatly consistent. Here's how they measure up.

AMERICAN DESIGNATION	DIAMETER	BRITISH DESIGNATION	DIAMETER
2	.15"	–	–
–	–	2	.13"
4	.13"	4	.12"
5	.12"	5	.11"
6	.11"	6	.10"
7	.10"	7	.095"
7½	.095"	7½	.09"
8	.09"	8	.085"
8½	.085"	–	–
9	.08"	9	.08"

The L.C. Smith Safety System

Several readers have written to me over the years asking whether the fact that the safety buttons of their older L.C. Smiths will move both forward and backward, and that the guns will fire either way, is a malfunction.

It is not. From about 1892 to 1914, the standard L.C. Smith safety was a three-position affair, on-safe in the middle, off-safe both forward and backward. The difference is that when you push the thumb piece forward, it's an automatic safety—that is, it automatically clicks back to "safe" when you move the top lever. Pull the thumb piece backward and it stays off-safe till you move it manually. Most bird hunters prefer automatic safeties, while target shooters like the manual kind; with an old-style Smith you could have it both ways.

Slam-Firing

Others have written to ask what "slam-firing" means. It means that if you pull the trigger and hold it, a Winchester Model 12 will fire when you jack the slide forward and chamber a cartridge. This is also sometimes called "fan-firing," on the same order as "fanning" a Colt Peacemaker. It is not a malfunction; it's the way the sear linkage was designed. Unfortunately, it also makes accidental discharges all too easy. Good as it is otherwise, I don't recommend the Model 12 for inexperienced shooters.

Browning, however, redesigned the system so that its Model 12s, built a few years ago as limited-edition 20- and 28-gauges, will not slam-fire.

Pump Guns

If you've ever dry-fired a pump gun and then found the slide stuck and the action impossible to open, you discovered something that most pump shooters, even those who've used them for years, never realize.

A pump-gun's breechbolt is locked when you fire it and stays that way till you push the slide-handle forward. John

Browning invented this feature a hundred years ago, as part of the Winchester Model 97, and so far as I know it's been used in every pump gun made since. The purpose, of course, is to make sure the action stays closed until the shot charge is out of the barrel. This was a problem with the Winchester Model 93, which Browning also designed, and he solved it with a mechanism that requires a slight forward push to unlock the bolt.

It's a brilliant idea, because you naturally push forward as a gun recoils after firing, so you'd never know it works that way unless you drop the hammer on a dud cartridge, an empty chamber, or a snap cap.

MOVEABLE TRIGGERS

The moveable trigger, one you can slide forward or back to make the blade easier to reach, is one of the refinements that came along as gunmakers developed guns specifically for sporting clays. Naturally seeking to make the most of an innovation, some makers claim this is a means of adjusting the length of pull.

It is, but then again, it isn't.

We measure stock length from the trigger to the butt, so moving the trigger forward or backward does change the actual measurement. But this can be misleading, because with a gun that has a full-pistol grip, which virtually every target gun does these days, the grip itself determines what I would call the effective length. In practical terms, the trigger is only a point of reference; where you actually grip the gun is the key element in determining proper stock length, because you want the base of your trigger-hand thumb far enough away from your nose that you don't whack yourself in the snoot every time the gun kicks back. The shape of the grip, in turn, determines to a great extent where you hold the gun, especially a full-pistol. In that case, the only way to alter the effective length is by adding, or subtracting, at the butt-end.

Sliding triggers do accommodate the size of your hand and the length of your trigger finger, which is good, but that's their only advantage.

MORE SHOTGUNS AND SHOOTING

and the length of your trigger finger, which is good, but that's their only advantage.

WD-40 AND GUNS

WD-40 is excellent for uses that require a penetrating lubricant where accumulated residue is not likely to cause problems, but that doesn't apply to guns. WD-40 is composed of some slick substance in particle form suspended in a liquid carrier; I don't know if it's silicone or Teflon or what, but I do know that when it's allowed to stand, the suspension precipitates and adheres to whatever surface it's on. You wouldn't notice it on blued or case-colored gunmetal that you wipe down, but it'll be quite apparent on polished internal parts. It looks like tarnish, though a soft wire brush will remove it readily. Over time, it can accumulate to the point of clogging close-fit bearing surfaces in locks, ejectors, and single triggers till the parts can't move.

If you want the final word on the matter, ask any highly skilled gunsmith. For the record, I called two of the best I know and asked what they thought about using WD-40 on guns. Abe Chaber said, "I recommend that my customers never use it. The deposit it leaves is not good for fine guns." David Trevallion told me a half-dozen horror stories about guns so gummed up with WD-40 residue that they were all but inoperable and wound it up by saying, "The bloody stuff can even gunk up V-springs till they won't compress."

The purpose of lubrication is to reduce friction, not to reduce tolerances that are minimal to begin with, but that's what WD-40 does.

A GLOSSARY OF COMMON ABBREVIATIONS IN GUN ADS

A&D	Anson & Deeley boxlock
AE	automatic ejectors
ANIB	as-new, in box
Bbl	barrel or barrels
BL	boxlock
BLE	boxlock ejector

254

BT	beavertail fore-end
Cased	comes with some sort of hard case
CB	checkered butt
CC	case-hardening color
Cyl	cylinder bore
DHBP	dog's-head buttplate (Parker)
DT	double triggers
Eng. stock	straight-hand stock
Ej	ejectors
Ext	extractors
F	full choke
FE	fore-end
IC	improved-cylinder choke
IM	improved-modified choke
LOP	length of pull
LT	long pistol-grip tang (Browning)
M	modified choke
MC	Monte Carlo comb
Mod	modified choke
NE	Nitro-Express
NEJ	non-ejector
NIB	new, in box
O&L	oak-and-leather case
O/U	over-under double
PG	pistol-grip
RF	refinished
RK	round-knob half-pistol grip (Browning)
SxS	side-by-side double
SBT	single-barrel trap gun
Semi-BT	semi-beavertail fore-end
Semi-PG	semi-pistol grip
SG	straight grip
Sgl	single barrel
Sk	skeet choke
Skt	skeet choke
SL	sidelock
SLE	sidelock ejector

SLNE	sidelock non-ejector
SN	serial number
SPG	semi-pistol grip
SPL	splinter fore-end
SST	selective single trigger
ST	single trigger
SR	solid rib
UL	underlever
VR	ventilated rib
XF	extra-full choke
¼	quarter choke (English)
½	half choke (English)
¾	three-quarter choke (English)
2"	2-inch chambers
2½"	2½-inch chambers
2¾"	2¾-inch chambers
3"	3-inch chambers
3½"	3½-inch chambers

ANOTHER WAY TO READ A GUN AD

You see them all the time in ads and dealers' lists, those little abbreviations that amount to a shorthand version of the language of guns:

CALABI & STUART 20-ga SxS SLE,
27" bbl, 2¾", IC&Mod, SG, DT, SPL, 85% CC,
14" LOP, CB.....$3750.

Because you know the lingo, you recognize this 20-bore Calabi & Stuart (a well-known Polish maker) as a side-by-side sidelock ejector gun with 27-inch barrels choked improved-cylinder and modified, 2-inch chambers, a straight-grip stock, double triggers, splinter fore-end, a 14-inch length of pull, and a checkered butt. About 85 percent of its original case-hardening colors still show.

Straightforward enough, right? Or maybe not. If you've spent much time fooling around in the gun market you've probably noticed that some, shall we say, discrepancies crop up now and then when you compare an actual gun with its description, and perhaps you've taken this to mean that the seller has done a bit of creative writing, taken some poetic license to embellish the appearance of a somewhat less attractive reality.

Not necessarily. The fact is, some of the standard abbreviations have more than one meaning. PG doesn't always mean "pistol-grip," and VR can indicate something other than a vent rib.

If you've read a lot of ads and looked at very many guns with an eye toward buying, you've probably suspected this for a long time. Well, it's true. Not that I'm out to become the *National Enquirer* of the gun world, or even the North American sporting version of the British *Sun*, but I feel it's high time the truth was told. So here are some of the more common abbreviations and what they might also mean:

SG "Sorry gun"
VR "Very rusty"
SR "Sorta rusty"
O/U "Outstandingly ugly"
SxS "Stocked by simpleton"
AE "Awful engraving"
DT "Doubles every time"
ST "Some termite damage"
SST "Some serious termite damage"
BL "Badly loose"
CB "Corroded bores"
PG "I got it for almost nothing from a pregnant woman who didn't have a clue what it was worth."
NIB "Nicks in barrels"
ANIB "Awful nice, if you're blind"
IC "Insides corroded"
BT "Just thought you might like to know what my secretary looks like."
LOP "Lame old piece"
MOD "Much obvious damage"

SPL   "Several parts lost"

SPG   "Shoots pretty good"

SLE   "Sticky left ejector"

Bbl   "Both barrels lousy"

Ext   "Engraving extremely tasteless"

CC   "Crummy condition"

DHBP (Parkers only)
    "Doggy, hacksawed, and badly pitted"

LTRK (Brownings only)
    "Lousy trigger, really kicks"

XF   "Extremely fragile"

Cyl   "Cover your longjohns, 'cause you're gonna get gunched if you buy this turkey."

Now if you sent somebody a fat check for the gun I described at the beginning and got upset because it wasn't what you expected, go back and re-read my little ad using this glossary. And next time, don't be too hasty in thinking you've been ripped off. Maybe you just weren't reading it right.

SOME THINGS
I'VE LEARNED

Several years ago, one of the magazines I write for ran a list of twenty things a hunter or fisherman should do in his lifetime. A few of the suggestions were mine, and in thinking about it afterwards, I decided to build a column around a list that was entirely my own.

The more I thought about it, though, the more I realized that should-do's are things somebody's done that turned out to be pleasant or poignant or otherwise significant—things learned, in other words.

But not everything we learn is necessarily pleasant, even when poignant or significant, so in the end I decided to take a slightly different tack and make up a list of some things I've learned in the forty years I've been a bird hunter. Not all of them are should-do's, by any means; some, in fact, are better filed under the heading I Hope it Never Happens to You. But it's real stuff.

How to ensure that almost everybody in a hunting party gets a good laugh and nobody gets many birds: Introduce to your cadre of dogs one female that no one knows is in heat.

How to bring about dead silence at breakfast in a hunters' cafe: Announce loudly, "Hell, I can't hit them quail. They run too fast!"

How to get the most aerobic benefit from a day's hunting: Be the only one in the group with a game pocket in your vest or coat.

Weird science: If you leave them alone, old female bird dogs can go for an ungodly long time without having to pee, especially if the weather's cold or rainy. But hole up in a country motel or someplace where you're available as a doorman, and their bladders shrink to the size of peanuts.

The perfect gift for a companion who screams incessantly for his dog's attention: A whistle, surgically implanted in his throat.

How to be someone's short-term companion: Scream incessantly for your dog's attention.

How to be someone's long-term companion: Respect the game, have a sense of humor, love your dog, and show all three without reservation.

How to get a lot of attention in a tavern on a hunting trip in Texas: Observe in a loud voice, "Y'know, if there was a back door in the Alamo, there wouldn't be a Texas!"

The most perfect gun ever built: The one that belongs to someone else.

The two things a traveling bird hunter needs most: A gun case by Americase; a travel agent who knows how to get things done and doesn't quit till your itinerary is the best it can be.

One time when character really shows: When you've missed six easy shots in a row and your partner hasn't.

Another time: When the situation is reversed.

Two different words that mean the same thing: Sportsman. Gentleman.

Two more: Dog. Love.

Nothing smells better than: A just-fired paper cartridge case. The Minnesota woods in October. Your partner's pipesmoke.

A freshly shot grouse, quail, prairie chicken, or woodcock. Rain in the woods. Winter. Wet dogs getting warm. Puppies.

Nothing tastes better than: Fried eggs and country ham at sunrise. Southern-cooked quail. Roast duck á la Dave Maass. Woodcock in sour cream. Ruffed grouse.

A sandwich made of coarse-grained bread, peanut butter, and onion, bacon, banana, or raisins, eaten after you've walked all morning long.

The first sip of whiskey after the dogs are fed and bedded, the birds and guns are seen to, and you've taken off your boots. In my case, this means Maker's Mark bourbon, Laphroaig, Lagavulin or some other Islay malt Scotch that tastes like seaweed marinated in iodine, which is a flavor not everyone likes—or as Tom Davis put it after trying Laphroaig at my suggestion, "Now I know why Hadrian built the wall; people who'd drink this are capable of anything."

Pipesmoke. Please, no scolding about health or political correctness; I know all about the one and don't give a damn about the other. The health risks of being a non-inhaling pipe smoker (which I'm not but I'd hope you would be) are about the same as breathing the automobile-exhaust fumes where you live, and a whole lot more pleasant. Cigars are in big-time these days and good cigars are okay, but the best ever rolled can't hold a candle to a pinch of well-blended tobacco fired up in a good briar pipe with a grain like a fine gunstock.

(And as a side benefit, ladies who retch at the thought of cigar smoke often are enchanted by the smell of a pipe.)

Nothing sounds sweeter than: Wind ruffling prairie grass. Rain in the woods. Boots in dry leaves. Boots in wet leaves. Dog bells. Wings. Your partner's voice saying, "Good shot!" The bobwhite's covey call. Puppies, sleeping.

Nothing feels quite like: Opening day. A puppy's first real point or blind retrieve. Taking a clean right and left on a covey rise. Centering an incoming pheasant that's forty yards up. Ten-year-old boots. Going hunting on your birthday.

Outwitting a wily old grouse or cock pheasant who's given you the slip a couple of times before, making him flush right where you want him, and not pulling the trigger.

The spark in an old dog's eyes when his nose is full of bird-scent.

Sitting in the truck at the end of the last day of the season and watching snow begin to fall.

Coming home to a house warmed by a wood fire and someone who is genuinely delighted by the gift of a grouse feather, a sprig of bittersweet or gray dogwood, or an odd-colored stone you happened to find.

And with all that, nothing feels better than being a bird hunter.

INDEX

Printed in the USA
CPSIA information can be obtained
at www.ICGtesting.com
CBHW030733101124
17096CB00001B/2

9 781586 671471